100 IDEAS THAT CHANGED STREET STYLE

Josh Sims

Laurence King Publishing

100 IDEAS THAT CHANGED STREET STYLE

Josh Sims

Introduction

The very idea of 'street style' might soon come to be considered rather dated. Once the term suggested all those grassroots ways of dressing that were not dictated by the catwalks. It stood for the spirit of individualism that, in many respects, underpinned the dress of those who society deemed maybe not fashionable, but, what is better, certainly stylish. Indeed, the two worlds – the high fashion of Milan, Paris, London and New York, and the grittier, less polished but no less creative style of the street – were worlds apart. If the former emanated from the fashion capitals, the latter could make a street-style capital out of wherever it originated, be that Seattle or St. Petersburg, Manchester or Rome.

But what kept the two worlds apart – aspiration, money, status, the media – is doing so less and less. While the trickle-down effect – in which street style derives from the diktats of the catwalks – used to be dominant, there has since been an acceptance that, increasingly, the real style – more local, less publicized, not underpinned by huge financial interests – is found at street level. Style trickles up to the catwalk and is reimagined there as a high-gloss version that is tagged 'fashion' and made both rarified (for the designer market) and approachable (for the high street).

Sometimes it is those designers who are lauded as most outlandishly imaginative – the likes of Vivienne Westwood, John Galliano or Alexander McQueen, to name just three

Britons – who are most sensitive to what is happening in the real world around them. It cannot just be coincidence that their design flair is backed by a sensibility for being 'down with the kids', as they used to say.

The proximity of street style and more mass-market fashion is only likely to get more intimate, and this as a result of the deep social and technological shifts of the early twenty-first century. For one, the internet and ubiquitous digital photography have meant that reportage of what were once small, localized, almost cultish street styles is now rapid and global – leading some to suggest that the idea of the fashion trend as we know it may well be reaching its end. Trends no longer have the time to mature before they are dissected, disseminated and, arguably, destroyed by too much awareness of them. What happens in a corner of east London can be echoed in another corner of Tokyo or New York within weeks. Trends – which thrive, even just for a while, on difference and clanishness – are confronted with the fact that technology is making the world a much smaller place; too small, even.

Manufacturing technology has assisted in this shift too. Knowledge of a street style may be one thing; having ready access to its looks is another. But now, thanks to rapid sampling, super-fast manufacturing and cheap labour, mass-market fashion retailers are able to spread far and wide an ersatz version of the latest 'in' style – be that from catwalk or from street – in a matter of days. It is another reason why trends develop, expand, peak and burst much faster than they ever have in fashion history.

Is this a good thing? On the one hand, these changes suggest a kind of democratization. When the fashion industry began to commercialize street fashion, it was simply responding to a demand for a style that was unavailable to the customer either because he or she was in the wrong place, at the wrong age or not part of the right scene. These changes, arguably, have increased the possibility of pleasure in dress and so, in that sense, they can only be a good thing.

And yet these changes also suggest that the kind of street styles documented in this book will remain essentially historic. It is hard to imagine a new street style embraced with the passion and conviction – such that it becomes a way of life as much as a way of dress – that fuelled such profoundly influential subcultures as, for example, the zazous, Teddy boys, mods or goths. Given how society has fetishized youth and embraced the outsider as an aspirational character over more recent decades, it is easy now to forget just how groundbreaking these street styles were: to stand apart from the crowd through one's dress was to invite more than ridicule or raised eyebrows. It could invite violence.

But in sticking to their street style through thick and thin, its adherents shaped their identity, found a comradeship in shared sartorial leanings and, most importantly, challenged the societal status quo. Street style subcultures are, indeed, much more than the clothes that make them.

Perhaps the greatest triumph of the early, post-World War Two street styles remains with us, however. Certainly street style often encourages the style-aware to dress like their peers, perhaps creating a bonding force for good in an increasingly fractured society, in which the means of community-building seem ever more weakened, at least in today's metropolitan centres. But it can also empower the individual to dress as an individual. The genesis of any street style lies in the desire of an individual — or that of a small group of individuals — to be distinct, to be themselves. That seems a deeply human need and one that the breakneck pace of transmission of trends might not diminish, but might in fact, by backlash, encourage. Indeed, if all trends are now current all the time, somewhere or other, in one pocket of a town if not in another, someone or some group might be inclined to push against them, to find their own unique style. And who knows, that could be the making of another entry for a book like this.

A style of one's own

IDEA № 1
THE TEENAGER

The idea of the teenager has become so prevalent as to make it hard to imagine a time when it did not exist. Of course, people were aware of the transitional nature of the few years beyond 13 – in fact, in 1904 psychologist G. Stanley Hall completed and published his groundbreaking *Adolescence*, and soon after higher educationalists were referring to the 'teen' period.

ABOVE: *A teenage Beatle fan in 1964*

OPPOSITE TOP: *Bruce Davidson's photo of teenagers at Coney Island in New York City in 1959. The boy wears a pair of khakis, and example of the army surplus wear that flooded the market after World War II.*

OPPOSITE BOTTOM: *A shot from Ewen Spencer's 'Teenage' series, shot in Cornwall, UK, in 2000.*

Over the next few decades this newly identified group would distinguish itself not only by its label, but also by espousing the rebellious new ideas of the times: the questioning of the logic of war that teen soldiers expressed during World War I, for example; or the radical change in attitudes to sexuality and race that developed over the 1920s – and, increasingly, the group's distinctive approach to dress. Distinctive, that is, from their elders.

Traditional society had it that children transitioned to adulthood, and to conservative adult style, without breaking step; it was the 1940s that gave birth to the idea of the teenager, and a rabble-rousing teenager at that. Certainly the social conditions during World War II saw the younger siblings of soldiers cut off from older generations and finding their own voice for the first time, whether it was through the **zazou** trend in Paris, the zoot suiters' rioting in Los Angeles or, soon after, the **Teddy boys** in the UK. Each new teen clan has its own look, which is alien to its forebears, even when, as in these three instances, it is founded on a twist to traditional tailoring.

From the 1950s, certain teenagers consequently looked different to those that had gone before, wearing exaggerated styles that distinguished them from older generations, for whom their look often seemed faddish, extreme or inappropriate – even when it was just denims, T-shirts or saddle shoes – and, merely because it broke with convention, symbolic of trouble. The advent of **rock and roll**, the first teen superstars – the likes of James Dean, portraying teens in Hollywood hits – **coffee bars** and other teen-centric meeting places, and rising disposable income for the demographic all helped characterize the teen as a new breed.

Marketeers were less fearful than parents, understanding that a need for distinctively teenage dress might be parlayed into one for distinct everything, and that teens could, and would, be a powerful consumer group – one, indeed, that would be defined by shopping. Even in the early post-World War II years teenagers accounted for sales of 33 per cent of cinema tickets, 40 per cent of records and 33 per cent of cosmetics. ∎

Socks and mags and rock and roll

IDEA № 2
TEEN IDOLS

The manufacture of pop acts with appeal to teens may be a phenomenon most readily associated with the 1960s and 1970s – from the Monkees to the Osmonds and David Cassidy – but it began as soon as music for teens became a focus of record companies in the early post-World War II years. Frank Sinatra was the first singing teen idol, the heartthrob of countless American bobby soxers during the phase of Sinatramania in the 1940s.

Teenage bobby soxers wore a uniform of Shetland sweater, poodle skirt and thick white socks – which had replaced nylons during the war – rolled down to the ankle. These were the socks in which they danced to prevent their penny loafers or saddle shoes from damaging the floor of the school gymnasium in which dances were often held – and the socks that marked them out as members of the teen idol's gang.

And the idol was everything: a groundbreaking survey in 1945, dubbed 'Life with Teena' (a play on '**teenager**'), found that, candy and other foodstuffs aside, all of the bobby soxers' pocket money went on entertainment, notably movies and music. At the same time, the bobby soxers' more casual style of dress helped define the new teenage demographic.

Teen idols like Sinatra sold well because they commodified sexuality for these teens in a way that, with some deliberately provocative exceptions – such as crotch-swivelling Elvis Presley, shot for TV only from the waist up – the society of the times could accept. Small wonder the music industry was quick to cash in by manufacturing other wholesome, parent-friendly acts too. Frankie Avalon, for example, was the anti-Elvis.

Certainly some early acts appealed more for their image and looks than their talent, often carefully selected so as to be not much older than their audience – approachability and imitability being a key aspect of their appeal – and provided with songs that addressed their teen listeners' experiences. For others, style was as important as content, from Gene Vincent's leather jacket and trousers to Elvis's adoption of denims, even though he was said to hate wearing them because their blue-collar utility reminded him of his poverty-stricken background.

Fledgling television ensured the kind of reach only dreamed of by older performers, while new teen magazines, including the groundbreaking *Seventeen*, helped turn mere mortals into idols, and created the teen pin-up, underlining the importance of looks and style. Inevitably, many performers had careers that lasted only as long as their own youth.

By the 1980s, new media – and the manufacture of product for them – came to define the teen idol. Overnight global stardom was made possible by MTV and, later, the internet. Teen idols included Michael Jackson, New Kids on the Block, Tiffany, 'N Sync (whose Justin Timberlake got a double dose as a solo act) and Justin Bieber, each shaping their own fan fashion in turn. ■

LEFT: *A crowd of bobby soxers wait expectantly and rather excitedly at the Paramount Theater in New York in 1945. And they wait for one man – The Voice, Frank Sinatra. Song Hits magazine jokingly offered the girls 'anti-swoon' mints. They didn't work.*

ABOVE: *A Michael Jackson fan – dressed for the part – in Rotterdam, 1988.*

Fans of the Bay City Rollers – a hit teen band in the UK during the 1970s – show their love not only through the words of their banners but the adoption of the Rollers' signature tartan.

Fashion as resistance

IDEA Nº 3
THE ZAZOUS

Many might risk approbation, scorn and ridicule for their clothes. Few would risk a beating, imprisonment and potentially death. The zazous of German-occupied France (1940–44) did just that, taking the cues for their sense of style from their American jazz, swing and bebop heroes.

This was a time when jazz, along with much of the avantgarde, including contemporary art, was heavily suppressed by the ultra-conservative Nazis in Germany and, to a lesser extent, by the Vichy puppet government in France. Such arts, and those that followed them, were denounced as decadent, degenerate and even immoral: to wear certain clothing that announced your high regard for them was a form of youth resistance, and one that would eventually drive the zazous underground.

Akin to the zoot suiters of the United States, and sharing a style with the British Teddy boys of the 1950s, the culture of zazou was focused around dancing and the music that had been imported into France, and Paris especially, during the 1930s. It was then that American jazz musicians had flocked to the French capital, to partake of its then liberal attitudes to race and progressive arts alike. But, while springing from the music, the style of the zazous was expressed through clothing.

Men wore outsized, knee-length checked jackets – using an excess of black-market fabric that deliberately subverted wartime rationing – narrow, ankle-length trousers, thick-soled suede shoes and brightly coloured socks. Their hair was heavily oiled and worn long for the period; rival youth groups were known to attack a lone zazou and shave this off. A pencil moustache was often also worn. Outlandish sunglasses completed the look. Women, typically bottle-blond and heavily made-up, similarly wore heavy shoes, together with boldly patterned stockings, pleated skirts – also against the expectations of rationing – and especially wide-shouldered jackets.

Zazou – the name is said to come from an ad lib in a Cab Calloway song – was a dandyism of extremes, in which clothing notably exaggerated the human form. It was also on occasion more directly political: when Jews were forced by the authorities to wear a yellow star patch on their clothing, the zazous wore their own version, marking themselves as outsiders too, though self-appointed ones. ∎

Style as an art form

IDEA Nº 4

DANDYISM

The original dandies were no less outsiders to society than those who have affected dandyism since: men whose often obsessive, individualistic self-expression through clothing took them both beyond acceptable measures of vanity and societal ideas of what it meant to be well dressed.

The eighteenth- to nineteenth-century English courtier George 'Beau' Brummell – a man who would spend hours tying and re-tying a pile of freshly pressed cravats until the perfect shape was achieved, who would have the soles of his boots polished, who hired an additional glove-maker just to fashion the thumbs – was, for example, dismissed as a mere 'tailor's dummy'; and this despite his having a profound impact on male dress as a consequence of his ill-fated friendship with the then Prince Regent. It was Brummell who stripped back what until then had been a flamboyant, fanciful and colourful style of male dress to introduce a rigorously cut, body-hugging and dark style that prefigured the modern business suit.

A little later, the French poet Charles Baudelaire considered himself to be one of this small but influential group of men who had 'no profession other than elegance, no other status but that of cultivating the idea of beauty in their own persons', as he wrote. For the dandy, being known for one's style – and its decadent pursuit – became a form of celebrity. The dress itself conformed to no uniform. Rather, one's clothing turned oneself into a one-off artform, utterly individualistic – sometimes theatrically so, sometimes with immense restraint.

Only unusual individuals affected a dandyism over the following century – to name a few, British poet Lord Byron, Irish writer Oscar Wilde, American socialite Evander Berry Wall ('King of the Dudes'), English humorist P.G. Wodehouse, Spanish artist Salvador Dalí, English essayist Max Beerbohm, English playwright and composer Noël Coward, and American author Tom Wolfe. The Congolese musician Papa Wemba epitomized the Congolese dandy style dating back to the 1920s, which he popularized in the 1970s and promoted with his Société de Ambianceurs et des Personnes d'Élégance. But dandyism as a philosophy of dress was arguably crushed by the advent of the massmanufacturing of clothing from the 1950s and, from the 1960s, the widespread wearing of (often unisex) casualwear.

During the 1990s, however, the appeal of dressing distinctively, and individually – which is to say, in opposition to trends – resurfaced again as a subculture, this time in Japan. It was defined by the wearing of hats (long after hats had fallen out of fashion for men), distinctive, highly polished shoes, accessories such as watch chains and canes, waistcoats, pocket squares, high shirt collars and ties, an appreciation for bold colour and pattern (such as checks and argyles) and, above all, tightly fitting tailoring. The look spread to London by the middle of the following decade, following a long revival of interest in bespoke tailoring. ■

ABOVE: *One of the pioneering dandies, Oscar Wilde (1854–1900), the Irish writer and wit. 'Only the superficial do not judge by appearances,' he once noted, a dictum he expressed in his own carefully measured dress.*

OPPOSITE: *Soho character, roué, raconteur, artist and dandy Sebastian Horsely, in his Soho, London, home in 2008. He died two years later.*

Aping one's betters

OPPOSITE: *Originally published in the Picture Post's story 'The Truth About the Teddy Boys' in 1954, this image shows a young Teddy boy outside the Mecca Dance Hall in Tottenham, north London, looking more elegant than confrontational.*

BELOW: *Style was as much an expression of group affiliation – us against them – as it was personal expression for the Teddy boys. Here a group of Teddy boys gathers in the street in North Kensington in 1956, shot by Ted documenter Roger Mayne.*

IDEA № 5

THE TEDDY BOY

'Birth of an "Edwardian". Teenage terrorists – absurd but deadly,' trumpeted one British magazine headline in the early 1950s. Its subject was Teddy boys, the first postwar British youth style tribe, mirroring the 'invention' of the teenager. Teddy boys, or Teds, were identified by their fastidious attention to a smart, suited look, a re-imagining of the tailoring style of their grandparents' Edwardian era (hence 'Ted', an abbreviation of 'Edward').

The magazine's sensationalist reaction reflects a moral panic at a – largely imagined – plague of juvenile delinquency. The Teddy boys' style, comprising a long jacket with narrow lapels, fancy waistcoat and narrow trousers, had actually been first adopted in the 1950s by upper-class men – and especially officers of the Guards, one of the more prestigious regiments of the British Army. It was a reaction against both the austerity measures imposed at the end of World War II and the influx of American style.

When the style was adopted by 'unrespectable' working-class youths, they were considered to be aping their betters, leading to so much disapproval that often only backstreet tailors would make the clothing for them. Taken a step further as the Teds did, the style looked like parody, with trousers a little too narrow – known as 'drainpipes' – waistcoats a little too fancy, crepe-soled 'brothel creeper' shoes, and a demeanour a little too spivvy, adding in American elements such as the Maverick tie and the heavily pomaded DA ('duck's arse') hairstyle. Teddy girls cut against the times' norms for femininity too, in boyish tailored jackets, rolled denims, carrying an umbrella more as accessory than out of need. This was expensive clothing as a means of youth in social revolt, before rock and roll made revolt fashionable.

Since a minority of Teds also carried flick knives or coshes, moved in intimidating, territorial gangs, tore up cinemas and developed a sometimes deserved reputation for criminality, the revolt was stoked up to be considered very real too – such that their dress could get Teds barred from certain establishments. For the majority, however, it was simply a question of British teens embracing their own style and shaping their own identity for the first time. ∎

Fashion follows the charts

RIGHT: *Elvis Presley (1935–77), the King and icon of rock and roll, at a recording session for RCA in 1956.*

BELOW *Rock and roll's self-expression was not simply a matter of style or a shared passion for the music – the dances, intimate and acrobatic, were just as liberating.*

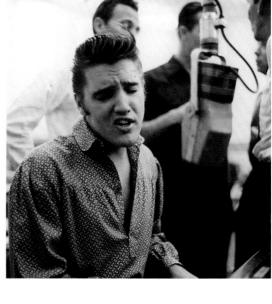

IDEA Nº 6

ROCK AND ROLL

When Elvis Presley sang about 'Blue Suede Shoes' in 1956 it was important for more than simply being one of the first hits of rock and roll, fusing country and blues, white music and black. Presley was also making a statement against the conservatism and conformity of the older generations that rock and roll was rebelling against.

Performing the song on *The Steve Allen Show,* Presley drove the point home, wearing black tie but also, as he put it, 'something that's not quite right for evening wear' – his blue suede shoes. Indeed, rock and roll was more than the music. It helped define the idea of the teenager as a life stage in its own right, with its own outlook, tastes and styles. Early rock and rollers the likes of Little Richard, Jerry Lee Lewis and Gene Vincent, and, in the UK, Cliff Richard and Adam Faith, had a

direct impact on the clothing worn among fans (not to mention their hairstyles, choice of transport, even slang).

The clothes defined an attitude of which parents and authority figures largely disapproved, thereby serving to underline their appeal. Over subsequent decades, certain items gained iconic status, from denims to leather jackets, boot-lace ties to winkle-picker shoes. Television's early coverage of rock and roll, through such pioneering teen

programming as Dick Clark's *American Bandstand* and *Ready Steady Go!,* ensured that rock and roll fashion was widely disseminated. Elvis Presley, for example, brought his own style to the stage – one shaped in large part by Memphis clothier and haberdashery Lanksy's, which would also outfit Carl Perkins and Johnny Cash. Much as rock and roll seemed to twist familiar forms of rhythm and blues music, so Presley twisted the conservative dress of the time: sharp suits just a little looser than normal, shirts but with the collar just a little higher, or turned up, trousers pegged and tighter than the norm. It was subtle subversion rather than outright rebellion that teen fans could emulate without being grounded.

In fact, 1950s rock and roll was the genesis of the connection between (teen) fashion and music, the latter arguably being the single most important influence in shaping style, especially at the street level: where Presley led, other groups and rock music movements followed, be that the Beatles' Nehru-collared jackets and Cuban-heeled 'Beatle boots' – designed by Anello & Davide in London – during the 1960s, the **glam** rock influence of Slade and David Bowie during the 1970s, **New Romanticism** during the 1980s or the Seattle sound and style of **grunge** during the 1990s. ■

Bill Hayley & His Comets, performing on the Thank Your Lucky Stars *TV show in Birmingham, UK, in 1964. The outlandishness of the act – with Al Rappa standing on his double bass – belied the fact that Bill Hayley, with his conventional suit and kiss curl, actually helped bridged the gap between pre- and post rock and roll generations.*

'Film-makers were highly aware of the lucrative teen audience.'

Big-screen teen scene

OPPOSITE: The drive-in, that quintessentially American experience – here near Flora, Illinois, in 1960 – was as much an opportunity to socialize and show off one's style in clothes and cars as it was to see one's teen hero in action on the big screen.

BELOW: Cinema targeted at teenagers continued to help define young style into the 1980s, as with the so-called Brat Pack of St.Elmo's Fire (1985), starring Andrew McCarthy, Emilio Estevez, Judd Nelson and pin-up Rob Lowe.

IDEA № 7
TEEN CINEMA

The portrayal of teenage life in the cinema had been happening long before the idea of the teenager was formed. In the pre-World War II decades, such films as *Broken Blossoms* (1919), *Stowaway* (1936) and *Love Finds Andy Hardy* (1938) helped make stars out of Lillian Gish and Mary Pickford, whose on-screen adolescent troubles were among the first to echo those of the audience. Similarly, the so-called flapper films of the 1920s had tackled rebellion and experimentation with drugs, foreshadowing the high-school films of the 1950s, when 'teen cinema' is more widely regarded as having begun.

Certainly it was with the postwar era that movies began not only to reflect teenage life – becoming the leading medium in seeking to do so with accuracy – but also to help define it, in attitude as much as style. *The Wild One* (1953), *Rebel Without a Cause* (1955) – among other movies tackling the idea of the juvenile delinquent – *The Blackboard Jungle* (1955) and *High School Confidential!* (1958) all helped mould the teen idea of cool, from Marlon Brando's biker jacket to James Dean's red blouson and denims, while *Gidget* (1958) had a pioneering setting amid the then new **surf culture**. Other style-led teen genre films were popular too, including hot-rod movies such as *Joy Ride* (1958) and the more sexual-ized rock movies, such as *Go, Johnny, Go!* (1959). By this time film-makers were highly aware of the lucrative teen audience.

Indeed, the teen or coming-of-age experi-ence was the focus of movies throughout the later twentieth century too, seeing a heyday in the 1980s. *Fast Times at Ridgemont High* (1982), *Sixteen Candles* (1984), *The Breakfast Club* (1985), *St. Elmo's Fire* (1985) and *Pretty in Pink* (1986) not only made **teen idols** of their stars, but the style of their so-called Brat Pack actors was reflected in teenage dressing, with a yuppie-meets-preppy elegant dishevelment. Baseball jackets, fingerless gloves, tweeds, big hair, turned-up collars, neckties worn with T-shirts in a kind of pre-hipster quirkiness – all made the transition from screen to street. *Fast Times* even helped make chequerboard sneakers by a company called Vans one of their all-time best-sellers. ■

The crucible of subculture

RIGHT: *The Festivalbar, in the Papalia on Viale America, in Rome in 1964. The two girls are reading cards to vote for which songs should be on the jukebox.*

BELOW: *Mods gather in a cafe in the West End, London, in 1964 – a place where ideas on the latest haircuts, or tailoring cuts, could be shared.*

IDEA № 8

COFFEE BARS

Forty years before global coffee retailers such as Starbucks revolutionized interest in coffee, shaped the look of city main streets and even changed habits of work and social lives – making the coffee shop a place to work remotely and an alternative meeting place to bar or pub – the coffee bar was a fixture of youth culture.

In the UK, coffee bars mimicked the culture already well established in, above all, Italy, by becoming a hub for teenage interaction. They were a place for teenagers to have a life of their own outside home. As one teenager said in a British Pathé film shot inside Soho's Le Macabre coffee bar in 1958: 'This is us, see, we're today – if you don't dig us shoot away to some square joint with the rest of the creeps.'

The same attitude would pervade such meeting places internationally over coming decades – from the North Beach hang-outs of the **Beat Generation** in the US, to the Rive Gauche cafes of Paris. The appeal was widely similar too. Coffee bars, and like venues, were accessible to all: they were cheap, well lit, female-friendly and, in the UK at least, did not serve alcohol. They were also open late. They were independent and individualistic (sometimes even amateurish) at a time when, again, in the UK, many youth clubs were controlled by either schools or church associations. With the installation of new imported Gaggia espresso machines, and with modern decor, they were fashionably continental in style and mood – a progressive update on the tea houses of the prewar age and a decidedly colourful counter to postwar gloom. And, crucially, they were typically fitted with a jukebox, so it was the norm to go to a coffee bar as much to dance as to sip an exotic cappuccino. The coffee bar was where trends were initiated, new fashions shown off, where subcultures – Teds, **mods**, **rockers** and beatniks alike, though not at the same time – congregated, where bands that would further shape street fashion were discovered. It was in London's Fantasie coffee Bar that Mary Quant planned the opening of her first boutique.

Indeed, British rock and roll can be said to have started in coffee bars too. In Liverpool, in northwest England, the Beatles met at a coffee bar that would later become the Jacaranda Club, owned by the band's first manager. Cliff Richard, Marty Wilde and Tommy Steele were among fledgling acts that performed at the 2i's, the Cat's Whisker, Moka (opened by Italian 'sex bomb' Gina Lollobrigida) or other coffee bars that sprang up in London's Soho during the late 1950s and 1960s. The Cat's Whisker is said to have had one of the first jukeboxes in the UK and to be where the hand-jive dance craze originated, as a means of dancing in a room too crowded to move one's feet. ■

The Rolling Stones' Mick Jagger and Brian Jones leaving Peter's Café in London, in the early 1960s. For Jones the street has become catwalk, a chance to show off his suit to waiting paparazzi.

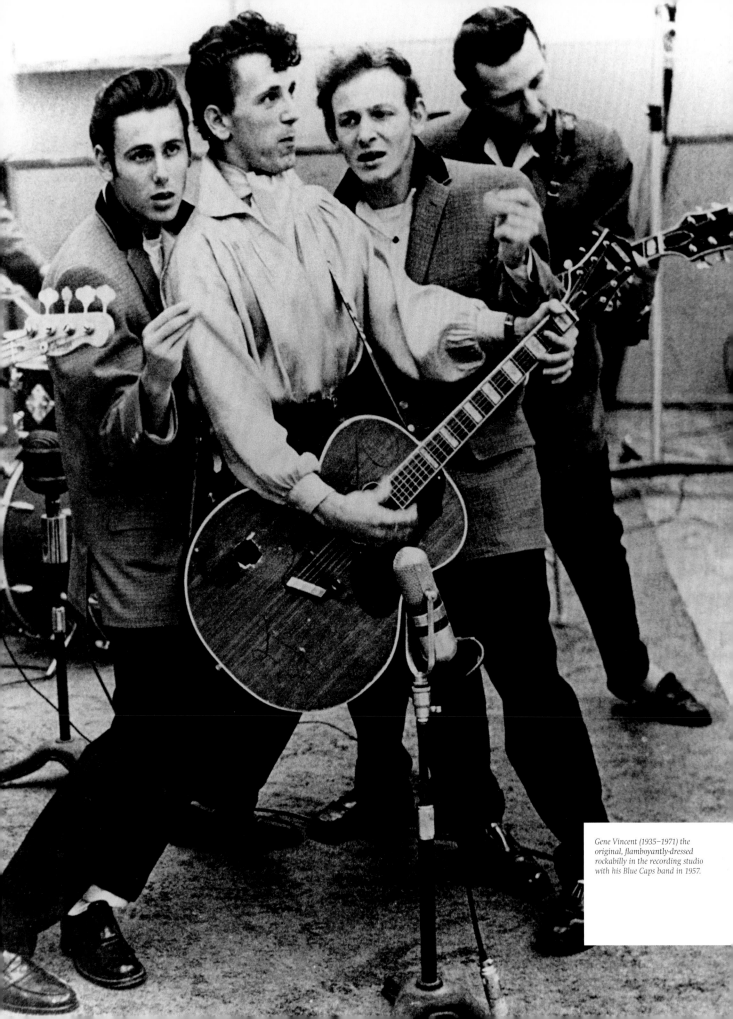

Gene Vincent (1935–1971) the original, flamboyantly-dressed rockabilly in the recording studio with his Blue Caps band in 1957.

Americana writ large

IDEA № 9
ROCKABILLY

If the post-World War II climate in America was still essentially conservative, rock and roll was naturally dynamite. But before Elvis Presley, Little Richard or Jerry Lee Lewis tore up the rules that said that teenagers were, culturally and attitudinally, just adults-in-waiting, there was rockabilly.

During the late 1940s and early 1950s the music genre played by the likes of Carl Perkins and Bill Haley fused the styles of rock (as nascent as it then was), R&B and country boogie music (also known perhaps pejoratively as 'hillbilly', hence the conflated name). The music created a dividing line between generations that until then had been blurred. Those three influences brought with them, similarly, a difference in dress from the traditional, sober look of the period: part historical, part flash, part Betty Page pin-up, part gaudy pulp novel – rockabilly style was the Americana of cowboys and pioneers by way of the stage.

At its more subtle this meant that young men and women wore more pop versions of adult looks of the period: the men in simple shirts and jackets, made from the synthetic wonder-fabrics being developed, such as rayon and viscose, and worn with the staple style of denims with characteristic turn-ups; the women in full-skirt dresses, full-skirted crinolines and flat shoes, with their hair up in ponytails. Its more extreme, nonconformist incarnations, however – notably during the 1980s and 1990s – would over subsequent decades come to define the American style of the period in all its colour, vivacity and optimism, indelibly associated with the diner and the drive-in movie.

Menswear embraced colour – even such 'feminine' colours as pink – pattern and novelty prints (notably those that reflected the atomic age), fabric with effects such as two-tone, western shirts and **jeans**, but also matching shoes and leather jackets and engineer boots borrowed from **biker** and hot-rodding cultures. Hair was longer and heavily oiled or Brylcreemed. Rockabilly women, similarly, shunned the understatedly or gently feminine for the overtly so: red lips and pencil skirts, peroxide hair, fringes and headscarves, tight sweaters, stockings and stiletto heels. Such elements would later play a part in the revival of **burlesque**, as well as, in exaggerated form, in the international rockabilly revival of the 1980s and 1990s. ∎

The outlaw aesthetic

IDEA Nº 10
BIKER CULTURE

Since the 1950s bikers, with their black leather jackets and heavy boots, have been characterized as living outside societal norms – self-proclaimed outlaws. The clothing, styling and iconography of bikers in the United States have been negatively associated with rebellion and antisocial behaviour, but also with freedom, self-determination and 'dropping out' – the life on the road as the two-wheeled itinerant.

The biker look that grew up after World War II incorporated practical, rolled jeans, heavy, buckled biker/engineer boots, T-shirts and denim jackets – rugged, tough, working-class clothes that distinguished their wearers from the 'men in grey suits' of conservative middle America. And most characteristically, of course, the black leather biker jacket, first designed by American manufacturer Schott at the behest of a Harley Davidson dealership. Black leather, of course, had connotations of fetishism and fascism that only added to the biker's outsider status.

Many bikers in the United States wore a patch on their leathers proclaiming themselves a '1%er'. The badge goes back to the Fourth of July weekend of 1947, when a 4,000-strong motorcycle rally descended on the small town of Hollister, California. The press, both locally and nationally, sensationalized the ensuing minor disruption as the 'Hollister riot'. Approached for comment, the respectable American Motorcycle Association allegedly responded by saying that 99 per cent of all motorcyclists were law-abiding, meaning that the last 1 per cent were outlaws (the AMA denies it made this statement, but it has nevertheless passed into biker mythology).

Almost inevitably, numerous bikers – many of them GIs returning from the war, keen to re-experience a sense of comradeship, with many no doubt also drawn to the adrenaline – presented themselves as allied to the 1 percenters; in doing so their mode of dress would, appealing to those who wore it, come to signal danger to those in society's mainstream. Biker gear would suggest the bad boy that might not necessarily be beneath. Some, however, would go on to form biker gangs, most famously the Hell's Angels, which – frequent despite its members' protestations that its reputation was the product of stereotype – did seem to operate outside of the law.

Popular culture perpetuated the public perception of bikers as untrustworthy and antisocial, most notably in 1953 with the film *The Wild One*, in which Marlon Brando played the disaffected leader of a biker gang ('What are you rebelling against, Johnny?' he is asked. 'What have you got?' comes the reply). Henceforth, the notion of bikers as twentieth-century cowboys, always on the wrong side of the sheriff, was sealed, in a form of American anti-hero myth-making. The 1960s saw a spate of biker movies, from *Cycle Savages* to *Easy Rider* (both 1969). Brando's image from *The Wild One*, with his sideburns, leather jacket and tilted cap, remains an icon of biker style. ∎

A Hell's Angels biker at a concert ay
Bath Festival in Britain in 1970, the
wooden hammer tucked into his belt
was not a style accessory.

Speed as style

IDEA № 11
THE ROCKER

If biker culture in the United States aspired to the itinerant life on the road , the so-called 'leather boys' of London in the 1950s were the embodiment of speed and aggression. Rockers, as they were eventually dubbed, rejected what they took to be the creeping effeminacy of late 1950s and early 1960s male fashions in favour of a look that was hard, dark and overtly masculine. Indeed, it would become the template for civilian sartorial machismo.

Nonetheless, despite rockers being turned into folk devils by exaggerated media reports of clashes with mods in British seaside towns, brawling was not an integral part of the agenda of the 'coffee bar cowboys' or 'ton-up boys' ('doing a ton' was slang for the 100mph, or 160km/h, speeds they aspired to), as they were initially known. The rockers were more interested in their motorcycles and their rock and roll.

Despite the film's being banned in the UK for 15 years, the cue to adopt a uniform may have come from Marlon Brando as outlaw biker Johnny in *The Wild One* (1953). Certainly Johnny's peaked leather cap was much admired – unable to source an equivalent locally, British bikers might take to liberating and customizing a milkman's cap, similar in size and form but without the dark overtones. Until *The Wild One* rockers – obsessive motorcycle enthusiasts – more typically wore an assemblage of army and Royal Air Force surplus, including shearling-lined flying jackets. But while their clothing remained essentially practical – certainly the rockers were considered to be woefully out of fashion for the time – their later choice of denims, motorcycle boots, white scarves (after the practice of World War II RAF fighter aces, sometimes even replaced by a colourful nylon woman's scarf) and, above all, black leather biker jackets quickly became iconic.

The latter essential garment played on all of black leather's myriad associations, including the British rock and roll of Billy Fury, **fetishism**, even Nazism. These were made all the more overt thanks to the rockers' embellishments – not only badges and sew-on patches, but studs, looped chains and the piratical skull and crossbones. Rockers would also paint on details of their favoured motorcycle company, as well as references to rallies attended and even speeds attained. Small wonder that, while rockers in Britain had died out by the mid-1960s, by then their look had been mimicked in France by the likes of the 'blousons noirs' and in Sweden by the 'skinnknutte'. Wearing a tricked-up black leather motorcycle jacket remained the shortest cut to looking as hard as one could. ∎

Rockers at their London spiritual home, the Ace Cafe on the outskirts of London in 1963. The clothes, as important as they are, are always secondary to the motorcycles.

Pursuit of the new

THE MOD

Mod was a London scene predicated on difference, on one-upmanship and individualism, on being an outsider. And because there was no one uniform, it was hard for the press to identify mods as a tribe, which allowed them to stay underground for longer. But, as a culture, and a clique, it could not survive its tenets becoming merely part of everyday fashion – indeed, shaping everyday fashion for the next generation.

While there have been several mod revivals, the first, defining era of mod occurred in the late 1950s to early 1960s, when (mostly male) dressers turned away from the UK and towards the Continent, notably Italy, and the American Ivy League for their smart fashion cues. In direct contrast to the Teddy boys before them, who had looked to the past for inspiration, mods, as their name suggests, sought only all things modern. It was the first fashion based on the pursuit of the new. The hair was not short back and sides but a college-boy cut. Tailoring was not drape, like the Teds, but single-breasted, narrow-lapelled, fitted, vented; ties were narrow too, trousers slim, shoes chisel-toed. Tennis shirts, boating blazers, desert boots, Harrington jackets and shrink-to-fit Levi's jeans – much of it sold on the black market by American GIs still stationed in the UK – were all part of a more casual mod look.

The style was expensive and hard to come by; much was bought on the then-new system of hire purchase, and much had to be made to measure, which saw the working-class sons of London's East End Jewish tailoring trade lead the way. Coffee bars and then live music venues became hubs where styles would be shown off, and where modern jazz would be listened to, or American R&B or soul – whatever music was new. Customized (i.e. 'individualized') Italian bicycles and, later, scooters proved the ideal form of transport between venues. Parkas – in easy supply thanks to postwar US Army surplus – became a convenient means of protecting the mods' precious and carefully curated clothing while on the move.

Mod was constantly seeking this week's look. Influential mods, or 'Ace Faces', set different styles, albeit with twists unnoticed by the uninitiated. Women adopted mod style too; arguably mod introduced the idea of some clothing being unisex. More than that, however, it helped make both clothes-obsessiveness and individualistic (if still relatively conservative) dressing – particularly as distinct from one's forebears – socially acceptable. Mod opened the floodgates to allowing youth to dress as it chose.

When *Quadrophenia* was released in 1979 – the film of The Who's concept album – mod became a mainstream fashion phenomenon. High-street fashion brands launched mod lines; mod iconography – the RAF roundel, the Union Jack – was plastered over anything that would sell; the music industry attempted to launch new mod bands. Going mainstream, however, signalled the death of mod for anyone who was, or had been, a purist of what might be called a style philosophy. ∎

Cinema as national style

IDEA № 13

LA DOLCE VITA

By the end of World War II, Italy was a ravaged country, its industry decimated and poverty rife. Small wonder, perhaps, that the glamour of the native movie industry of the 1950s, together with the creation of a powerful celebrity culture, would prove so popular. The concept of bella figura (beautiful image), an impermeable shell of unruffled chic, found expression again, reborn on the silver screen.

The likes of Luchino Visconti's *Rocco and his Brothers* (1960) and Pier Paolo Pasolini's *Accattone* ('The Scrounger', 1961) would be of influence on subcultural trends over the following decades, creating a momentary vogue for the scruffy, working-class, white vest and worn flannel trousers style suggested by the latter film's name. But the defining film of the period – indeed, the film that defined a specifically Italian style internationally as much more polished, more chic – was Federico Fellini's *La Dolce Vita* (1960). So much so, in fact, that a black turtleneck sweater, as worn by leading man Marcello Mastroianni, is known in Italy as a 'dolce vita'. Through this movie, cinema proved itself a medium by which a national style could be forged. It also proved that an industry could not only be rescued but established on a global footing, in large part through the magnetism of its stylishness: the slick suits and sunglasses, the kitten heels, little black dresses, tight knee-length skirts and full blouses. Even the everyday moment was one to dress up for.

But while Italy's leading ladies of the time, including Sophia Loren, were dressed to reflect more international catwalk trends, it was Mastroianni who would become the figurehead for a characteristically Italian look. In *L'Assassino* ('The Assassin', 1960) and *Yesterday, Today and Tomorrow* (1963), for example, he wore a Bruno Piatelli-designed short, double-faced tweed coat – inside out, with the waterproofing on the inside – which became a national menswear standard; in Fellini's 8½ (1963) his character's funereal black suits, white shirts, plain black ties and dark sunglasses defined the minimalism of Italian menswear. The look helped to redefine Rome, Milan and Florence not only as world fashion capitals but also as stylish haunts for the Hollywood stars of the decade. ∎

The romance of the prairies

IDEA № 14
WESTERN STYLE

Inspired in no small part by the romantic iconography and mythology of the cowboy figure – as outsider, law-giver, traveller; as solitary, tough, self-sufficient and at one with his environment – many subcultures have taken elements of western dress and made them their own.

Denim may be by far the most ubiquitous example, whether in jeans or jackets, but this has not been the only element of traditional American western wear – those styles worn during America's pioneer years of the second half of the nineteenth century – to have resonance in fashion.

Its mythology has certainly appealed, but so has its ruggedness: this was practical, though often colourful, clothing for the great outdoors of the nineteenth century, before an era of smart base layers and technical fabrics. Perhaps its most famous item, the Stetson, evolved into its most recognized form as a result of decades of cow hands' modifications to make their hats more functional: high enough to keep the head cool, broad enough to keep the rain off, not so broad it would blow off, and so on.

Cowboy-inspired symbolism gained currency internationally as a result of Hollywood and the western movie genre from the 1920s onwards. In the pre-World War II decades stylized singing cowboy stars such as Roy Rogers, Gene Autry and Hank Williams were popular, while from the 1970s on American fashion giants such as Ralph Lauren have tapped into both a longing for a national style and a nostalgia for a history since overshadowed by urbanization and industrialization.

Biker culture, for example, has made the large buckled belt and leather waistcoat its own; **hip hop** and American **gang cultures** have borrowed the bandana; the shield-front shirt and the bolo or boot-lace tie became staple styles of **rockabilly**; and the fringed leather jacket has been a recurrent teenage as well as heavy metal trend. Individual items such as the Native American shawl, prairie skirts and cowboy boots have entered the mainstream, in part driven by interest in the likes of line-dancing and country and western music, one of the world's most popular genres. ∎

ABOVE: *The cowgirl look – brown suede chaps over jeans, plaid flannel shirt, long poplin coat, neckerchief, boots and broad-brimmed hat – formed part of the fall/winter 1978–79 collection from Ralph Lauren, the designer most influenced by classic Americana.*

BELOW: *The excess jewellery may be more gangsta or bling than country, but the faded denims, decorative belt buckle and boot-lace tie suggest that its anonymous wearer is more western than urban.*

Actor and singer Leonard Slye, better known as Roy Rogers, with his horse Trigger. Rogers (1911–1998) defined the commercialized idea of the cowboy, his exuberant and polished cowboy attire helping to market his movies, radio and TV shows and even a franchised restaurant chain.

School uniform as elite style

IDEA № 15
PREPPY

With the aspiration to mimic social superiors a driving force in much of fashion history, it was perhaps inevitable that men's style in the United States would look to the dress sense of the alumni of elite educational institutions for inspiration. With the American postwar consumer boom of the late 1940s and 1950s, this trend was exacerbated – and a so-called Ivy League style of dress was identified.

This was the uniform of those who attended prestigious East Coast WASP (White Anglo-Saxon Protestant) universities such as Princeton, Yale and Harvard, the alma mater of the nation's power brokers, and the preparatory (prep) schools that prepare children for them – from which the word 'preppy' derives. The northeastern climate also played a part in the look. The style incorporated khaki trousers, boat shoes, penny loafers, argyle sweaters, madras check jackets, piqué polo shirts, navy blazers, sack suits and button-down Oxford cloth shirts. Certain outfitters, including J. Press and Brooks Brothers, came to be the main purveyors of preppy style (with J. Press having stores on college campuses and Brooks Brothers inventing the button-down Oxford cloth shirt). The look was smart but casual and quietly expensive, embodying upper-class privilege and exclusivity – a world of country clubs, private golf courses, yachting and good connections.

So particular was the mode of dress that it became the stuff of stereotype and – with the social changes of the late 1960s and 1970s that saw the foregrounding of a **hippie**, anti-consumerist philosophy – even of ridicule. However, as with the consumer boom of the 1950s, that of the 1980s brought the revival of preppy style, though this time as a more distinct and more colourful fashion, spread through Brat Pack films such as *The Breakfast Club* (1985) and *Pretty in Pink* (1986) and shaped by American brands such as Ralph Lauren, Tommy Hilfiger and J. Crew. In fact, Arthur Cinader, the founder of J. Crew, launched his company on what he correctly predicted would be widespread interest in preppy fashion following the publication of Lisa Birnbach's best-selling *Official Preppy Handbook* (1980), which identified and gently satirized those who wore the style and lived the attendant lifestyle. ∎

TOP: *John F. Kennedy epitomized the preppy lifestyle of the East Coast WASP – relaxed, outdoorsy, moneyed and sportily dressed, here in polo shirt, khakis, white socks and deck shoes.*

ABOVE: *Although preppy was an essentially male style, women embraced its classic ease too. Here a student talks to classmates near an ivy-covered wall on the campus of Smith Collage, Northampton, Massachusetts in 1948.*

OPPOSITE: *Preppyish students gather near Harkness Tower, New Haven, Connecticut. The sack suits, button-down shirts, khakis and loafers made for a comfortable go-anywhere uniform.*

The body as canvas

TATTOOS

The nineteenth- to twentieth-century Western association of the tattoo with criminals, seafarers and deviants, rather than its more ancient history among different peoples, arguably made it a taboo there for the breaking. 'It is,' as American socialite said in the 1890s, 'the most vulgar and barbarous habit the eccentric mind of fashion ever invented'. Yet, from the 1960s, and more notably from the 1990s, to openly wear a tattoo was for youth a public statement of individuality, personal credo and adulthood – a symbolic break with the nest perhaps, rather than the bodily defilement their parents often considered it.

The permanency of tattooing also gave it a 'freakshow' credibility in the wider world of late nineteenth-century body art and modification of which it became an element, underlining the outsider connotations that, for example, once allowed circus entrepreneur P.T. Barnum to become a leading exponent of tattooed people for entertainment, hyping them with gory stories of abduction and forced tattooing.

The reasons for tattooing's late twentieth-century boom might include group membership, increased secular spirituality, pro-primitivism in a technological world, or a kind of personal branding. Some adopted tattoos as part of the early 1960s counterculture movement, Peter Fonda and Janis Joplin among them. By the 1980s tattoos were being driven both by visibility (media coverage of tattooed celebrities) and access (a huge growth in tattoo parlours). They were embraced by rap and hip hop communities, in turn by African-American sportsmen, from there by the wider street culture and finally, in the 1990s, by the youth-centric **celebrity** world. Tattoos in general not only became fashionable, but different styles also became subject to their own fashions: Chinese characters, Gothic type, 1950s **retro**, Sailor Jerry classic and so on.

Indeed, as with most outsider art forms adopted by youth, eventually tattooing came in from the cold to become mainstream, losing its subversiveness and winning greater recognition of its artistry. Tattooing is now supported by national conventions, a proliferation of thoughtful tattoo magazines, television shows and a saturation of the market for tattooists. New York City lifted a ban on tattooing only in 1997, while in 1999 one of its major cultural institutions, the American Museum of Natural History, hosted its first major retrospective on the subject. London's Victoria and Albert Museum is also attempting to establish a contemporary tattoo archive. The level of acceptance is perhaps best measured by the fact that tattoo style even became fashionable as a graphic device on merchandise, from handbags to pillow cases, for those who dared not have the real thing but liked the edginess the art form suggests. ∎

The invention of jazz cool

IDEA № 17
BLUE NOTE

When American jazz musicians of the late 1940s and 1950s performed, it was not only their music that was termed 'cool'. Their sharp, high-quality clothing itself reflected the laid-back, lighter, subtle sound of their music – as popularized by the Blue Note record label – and the apparently effortless ease of their playing.

Their clothes were the traditional, wide-shouldered suiting of the time, with an Ivy League feel that focused on crisp, bright-white button-down shirts, rep ties (striped ties said to be typically worn by sales representatives), plain white T-shirts, penny loafers, chinos and flannel trousers.

Miles Davis, Chet Baker, Bill Evans, John Coltrane, Gerry Mulligan, Charles Mingus and others were all dedicated, practised musicians, having given recitals since childhood for which they were expected to dress presentably. It was a habit that stuck. What these jazz masters wore, often as signatures, consequently attained an unexpected fashion credibility: Dizzy Gillespie's goatee, black horn-rimmed glasses and beret, Lester Young's tilted pork-pie hat, Davis's seersucker sack suits, club-collared shirts, bow-ties and Bass Weejun loafers. Much of it was bought from the Andover Shop, a small menswear store in Andover, Massachusetts, favoured by the jazzmen. The fact that many of them were black also gave the traditionally white Ivy League style a new twist.

Indeed, these jazz players in part invented the modern idea of **cool** that would later inform the performances of actors and style icons such as Steve McQueen and Paul Newman. It was Capitol Records that in 1953 helped popularize the term with its album *Classics in Jazz: Cool and Quiet*; Davis drove it home with his seminal *Birth of the Cool* compilation in 1957. By association with these performers and their performances – in smoky, ill-lit, intimate late-night venues, immortalized in evocative black-and-white photography – 'cool' came to be associated with the idea of an effortless style and nonchalant manner. ■

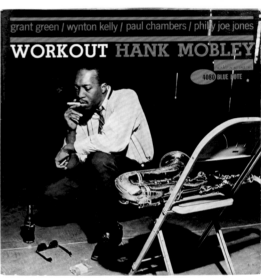

LEFT: *Chet Baker: white t-shirt, white socks, penny loafers, hair, trumpet, attitude.*

ABOVE: *The colour-toned or black-and-white but largely minimalistic design style of the Blue Note record label played its part in making jazz a style as much as a musical aesthetic.*

Trumpeter Miles Davis, in a sharp peak-lapelled, double-breasted chalk-stripe suit, ready for performance in West Germany in 1959. Note the patch pockets and one-button cuffs – both unconventional for a formal suit of this kind.

Intellectual cool

RIGHT: *French actress and singer Juliette Greco, during rehearsals for her two-week season of late night shows at the Globe Theatre, London, in 1969. The eyeliner and black polo neck were signatures of her graphic style of dress.*

BELOW: *Allen Ginsberg, Jack Kerouac and Gregory Corso, beat writers, in Greenwich Village, New York, in 1957, their clothes suggesting a new kind of urban intellectual.*

IDEA № 18

THE BEAT GENERATION

Thinking big thoughts or practising disdain for the humdrum mainstream of society may have become a standard activity in bars and cafes the world over – but it took the bohemians of the Left Bank area of Saint-Germain-des-Prés in Paris both to make it a job and to make it look good.

Inspired intellectually by existentialist philosopher Jean-Paul Sartre, and sartorially by the tailored classicism of the masters of American jazz, particularly early 1940s bebop – existentialism and jazz alike quashed by the Nazi occupation of Paris during World War II – the denizens of the Rive Gauche (Left Bank) came to define the dark, dishevelled, careworn style of chic intellectualism.

And that, in short, meant smoking endless Gitanes or Gauloises and wearing a great deal of black. The singer Juliette Greco, part of the postwar Left Bank scene, would claim that her wearing of black stemmed from poverty, that the mannish clothes she wore were hand-me-downs to compensate

for her otherwise sparse wardrobe, and that she found the fact that she was subsequently imitated rather amusing. She played on this idea of poverty – maybe based on truth, maybe all part of the pose – by often refusing to wear shoes.

The style reached its apex in the United States of the 1950s, when a more freewheeling, nonconformist group of artists – among them novelist Jack Kerouac, poet Allen Ginsberg and his muse Neal Cassady, and later songwriter Bob Dylan – coalesced around New York's Greenwich Village, expounding on radical (for the time) lifestyle choices such as drug experimentation, Eastern philosophy and a rejection of consumerism that prefigured the hippie movement.

The so-called 'beat generation' (as Kerouac called it) or 'beatniks' (as the press called it) took some cues from the Parisian wartime look: the jeans and denim shirts may have been quintessentially working-class American at the time, but the sandals and black polo-neck sweaters implied the same minimalistic, grungy detachment – detachment because for the beats the way they dressed was incidental to the art. It was non-fashion fashion. The press would actually influence the look inadvertently with the stereotype of the beatniks it portrayed, adding beret, goatee beard and bongo drums, which a few less self-conscious beats adopted in turn. ■

Beat writer Jack Kerouac at a party in New York in 1959. The crumpled mac played somewhat to the Beats' 'man of the people' image.

East copies West

STILYAGIS

Many style subcultures provoke the establishment; some set out to do expressly that. Few, however, while upsetting older generations, risk outright repression. Zazou in France of World War II was one. Just as striking were the stilyagi of the USSR, members of a style cult that seemed to embody the ideological clash between capitalism and communism.

Indeed, during the 1950s, its followers – men and women in their twenties, many of whom had experienced a taste of Western ways during the war – seemed to be a subversive, public, visual reminder that the Soviet state machine might not have all the answers when it came to lifestyle choices.

The stilyagi (loosely meaning 'the stylish' or 'style hunters', a term originally applied by outsiders as one of derision) would dress in ways that expressed admiration for the notably American youth culture of big band, swing and rock and roll. Their clothes reflected both a circumstantially narrow idea of that culture and, owing to the narrow range of options in dress available in Soviet stores, the difficulty of emulating it.

This often resulted in a look that would seem to Westerners to send up the American styles. Favoured among men were zoot-style long jackets, brightly coloured shirts, thin ties, thick brothel-creeper-type shoes, pompadour hairstyles and even adopted, Americanized nicknames, while women might wear full below-the-knee, tight-waisted skirts and tight sweaters. They called each other 'chuvak' and 'chuvakha' – 'guys' and 'girls'. One story has it that when the Leningrad Carriage Works launched a new, more plush and brightly painted tram in 1956, it was quickly dubbed the 'stilyaga'.

As with zazou, the sheer numbers of youths with stilyagi leanings meant it was a look the authorities, especially the official youth newspaper *Komsomol Pravda*, sought more to mock out of existence rather than physically act against. This was in no small part because stilyagi were typically the children of a wealthier Soviet elite. That said, those of them who made their own American-style music were, reportedly, imprisoned if caught. And gangs with more pro-state leanings would often viciously attack stilyagi and destroy their clothing.

Such repression declined, come the early 1960s, with a Soviet Union less consciously closed to Western influence. With it came something of a decline of the stilyagi, in part because by then its adherents were older, in part because they had, in a sense, won the right to self-expression. Perhaps also it was simply because, their outsider status diminished, the lifestyle no longer carried that spark of rebellion. ∎

Flesh as fashion

IDEA Nº 20
BODYBUILDING

Bodybuilding had been recognized as a form of exercise regime as early as the 1880s, even if its exponents were largely to be found in carnivals and circuses showing off their 'superhuman' strength. By the early 1900s national competitions formalized the niche practice, with 'physical culture' widely recognized by the 1930s.

But it was perhaps not until the postwar 1950s – with the advent of international competitions, a specialist press, nutritional supplements and the gym industry, not to mention a boom in superhero comics – that hefty muscle mass was appreciated more for its purely aesthetic appeal than its suggestion of manly strength. Charles Atlas's famed ads promised to make a 'new man' out of those who took his course, to turn 'weaklings into He-Men', suggesting to 'skinny' male readers that 'the best things in life' (including 'advancement in business' and 'popularity with others') may be passing them by for want of the fashionable body for the times. What you had under your clothes was as important as your wardrobe.

While the intensity of this idea fluctuated over the second half of the twentieth century, athletic bulk became a staple of the macho stereotype, attended by a steady emphasis on muscle definition. Certainly fashion, advertising, Hollywood and popular culture have each helped stress the much more toned physique as preferable to the generally large build of the masculine archetype of the 1960s and 1970s – and fashion has extended the opportunities to display that physique. The so-called 'muscle' or cap-sleeved T-shirt, with sleeves cut high to the shoulder, may have been perceived as a quintessentially male garment ever since Marlon Brando donned one to play Stanley Kowalski in the film version of *A Streetcar Named Desire* (1951).

But by the 2000s it had been joined by the deep-V T-shirt, technical stretch fabrics and a much tighter, body-hugging silhouette in menswear. While street fashion also embraced its opposite – the skinny, boyish, almost prepubescent nerd archetype – it was through the mainstreaming of bodybuilding via gym culture that the 'six pack' or the 'cut' body became the kind of style statement that could not be bought and which only time took away. ∎

Arnold Schwarzenegger, before he became a movie star and governor, in rather public bodybuilding mode in Munich, Germany, in 1967. The 'Austrian Oak' began weight-training when he was 15, and was Mr Universe by the time he was 20.

Free and easy living

RIGHT: *Max Bowman captures the Bohemian spirit of surf style in 1967, from the chunky cardigan and hippiesque necklace through to the white Levi's.*

IDEA № 21

SURF CULTURE

Surfing may not be an obvious cue for fashion, given its need for minimal clothing or, latterly, a wetsuit. But the activity has had huge resonance in wider popular culture, from music and movies to language and styles of dress. Surf style was, at its peak, self-consciously free and easy – loose-fit over-shirts (maybe a woollen Pendleton to warm oneself in when fresh from the sea), long shorts, perhaps longer hair too. It was a style that signalled a lifestyle one might not have, but aspired to.

RIGHT: *Max Bowman captures the Bohemian spirit of surf style in 1967, from the chunky cardigan and hippiesque necklace through to the white Levi's.*

Surfing, though normally associated with Hawaii, California and Australia, was devised by the ancient Polynesians some 3,000 years ago. The beginnings of the modern culture can actually be dated to the early twentieth century, when Hawaiian surf pioneer and Olympic swimmer Duke Kahanamoku introduced surfing from California to Australia in 1915. The first major surf competition was held in 1928. The advent of the affordable motor car around this time made surfing hotspots more accessible and helped spread the sport further, as did the technological developments of the next few decades (especially those made as part of the 1939–45 war effort), bringing in lighter, stronger, more stable boards.

But it is with the 1940s to the 1960s, surfing's golden age, that surf style is most strongly associated. High-waisted, lace-up board shorts were popularized by Kahanamoku, but it took a 'mom and pop' tailoring shop in Hawaii, M. Nii, to make the version – called Makaha trunks, after the Hawaiian surfing mecca – that would transcend the surfing community. Favoured by celebrity surfers Richard Boone and Peter Lawford, they would soon be photographed on Lawford's friend John F. Kennedy. Other brands caught on – sportswear company Jantzen, for example, struck the first endorsement deal with a surfer, Ricky Grigg, while Hang Ten devised fast-drying nylon shorts.

The appeal of the surf's easy, endless summer lifestyle soon spread among even those who never went in the water or, indeed, spent much time in the sun. When Elvis Presley starred in *Blue Hawaii* (1961), preparation for which saw him spending time under a tanning lamp, the Hawaiian shirt – the après-surf shirt of choice – attained widespread popularity. The same year saw the founding of the Beach Boys and their early hits – 'Surfin' Safari', 'Surfin' USA', 'Surfer Girl' – drove a genre of 'surf music', including the Surfaris and 'surf guitarist' Dick Dale. Surf culture's impact would endure: in 1984, surfboard maker Shawn Stussy launched a surf-inspired casualwear line that would shape the look of early **skateboarding**. ∎

'High-waisted, lace-up board shorts were popularized by Kahanamoku.'

The authenticity of the everyman

IDEA № 22
JEANS

Few items of clothing have become so globally ubiquitous as a pair of jeans. Indeed, jeans, or something like them, have been worn since the eighteenth century, when merchant sailors in Genoa (the origin of the word 'jeans') wore clothing made from a fabric woven in Nîmes (the origin of the word 'denim').

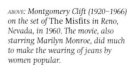

But it was in the late nineteenth century that jeans were first worn in their modern incarnation, largely by the frontiersmen of the California Gold Rush. They bought their denims – then sold as 'waist overalls' – from a certain Levi Strauss, who eventually patented the five-pocket design of a pair of jeans that would become the classic look (though the original model only had one back pocket). Strauss marketed his jeans on the basis of their strength: the label showed two horses attempting to pull a pair apart, while pocket corners were riveted in place, an idea Strauss bought from a tailor named Jacob Davis. Their hard-wearing nature has continued to be highly regarded, and jeans are one of the few garments in which an aged look is appreciated, even faked. For the same reasons of utility, jeans became the staple wear of cowboys and ranchers and the workers of twentieth-century American industrialization, later spreading to bikers and rock and rollers. Jeans embodied the romance of history, American history in particular.

It was the adoption of jeans by hero and social outsider archetypes, famously including Marlon Brando and James Dean, that gave denim the image of rebellion that, from the late 1950s onwards, made a pair of jeans the benchmark garment of youth. Jeans could be worn by hippies as much as by Hell's Angels outlaws, and anyone in between. Arguably, until the 1980s they were a garment, in fact, that people were expected to grow out of: jeans were not acceptable attire anywhere there was some form of dress code, unspoken or otherwise. That decade, however, 'designer denim' was introduced, by Calvin Klein among others – darker, crisper, smarter, and carrying a brand that suggested everything jeans had not been before: costliness, chic, formality.

Denim subsequently underwent constant, often radical evolution, retaining the appeal of its hardiness but now offered in myriad cuts, styles, colours and treatments, such as stone-washing and sandblasting. The wearing of denim has become increasingly ageless and less and less restricted by ideas of propriety. ∎

ABOVE: Montgomery Clift (1920–1966) on the set of The Misfits *in Reno, Nevada, in 1960. The movie, also starring Marilyn Monroe, did much to make the wearing of jeans by women popular.*

LEFT: Jeans of all hues and conditions, queuing in Paris in 2009. Look at any queue and jeans are likely to be the predominant trousers of choice.

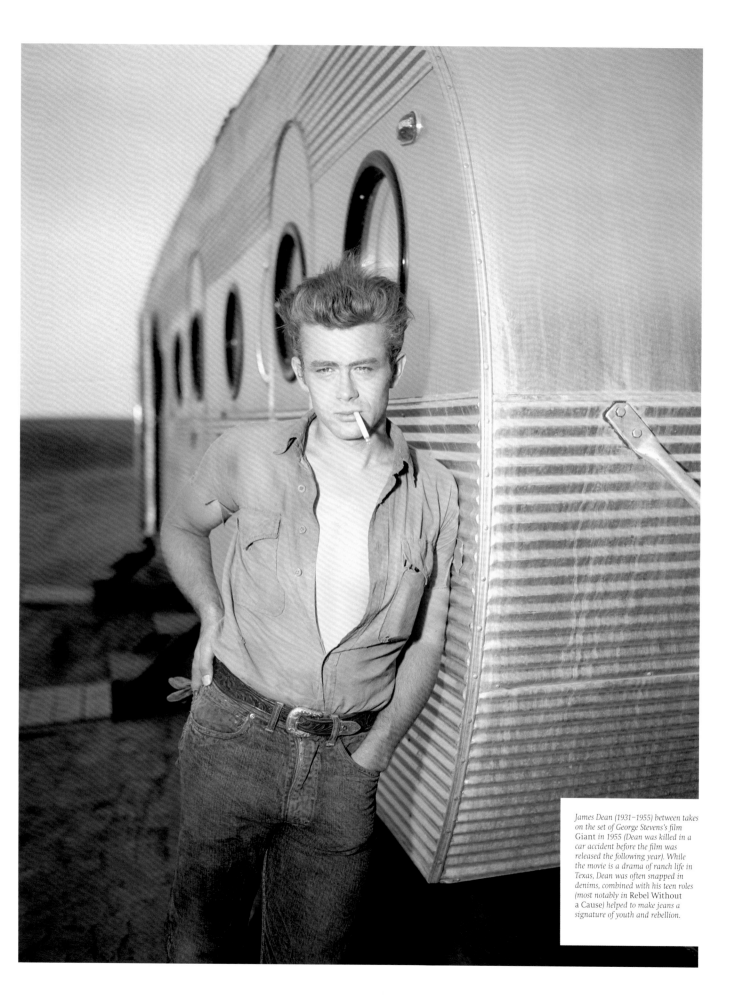

James Dean (1931–1955) between takes on the set of George Stevens's film Giant in 1955 (Dean was killed in a car accident before the film was released the following year). While the movie is a drama of ranch life in Texas, Dean was often snapped in denims, combined with his teen roles (most notably in Rebel Without a Cause) helped to make jeans a signature of youth and rebellion.

Who needs clothes?

NUDITY

Could not wearing clothes at all be a kind of fashion in itself? The hippies of 1960s West Coast America thought so (perhaps assisted by the climate), regarding a lack of clothes as less a style choice than a lifestyle choice or political statement. The flaunting of one's nudity in public became a form of protest, challenging social norms and supposedly conservative, constraining ideas of 'decency'.

For some, being nude was simply fun and liberating – sexually liberating, too. You were who you were, without the codes and conventions of clothing to muddle the message: this was essentially the idea held by active nudists both predating and post-dating the hippies. For others there was pleasure in the shock factor. And for still others it was a profound act. One hippie, quoted in the *Matrix* newspaper in 1968, noted that it was important for 'genitals to lose their special significance', because only then will people 'cease to fear them. It is

because they are hidden that they are ugly and dirty.'

Certainly most hippies' abandonment of clothing ran quite consciously counter to the prevailing ethos of the time – both in terms of the materialistic consumer boom by which advertising and popular culture were encouraging an ever faster turnover of style and an increase in the purchase of fashion items, and in terms of the way nudity or near-nudity was portrayed as nearly always highly sexualized, whether in ads or in big-selling magazines of the era such as *Playboy*.

Perhaps one style aspect of nudity did remain for the hippies, despite their lack of clothes. Once naked, the body became a blank canvas, and the painting of it – with 'peace and love' imagery, from flowers to psychedelic patterns to the symbol of the Campaign for Nuclear Disarmament – became part of the hippie look.

This is an idea that would be largely lost – short of the street festivals and football matches at which body and face painting took hold in the later decades of the twentieth century. Indeed, given societal conventions, embarrassment and climate, nudity was perhaps never going to become a big (if counter-intuitive idea) in fashion. Perhaps one consequence through the late twentieth century and early twenty-first century, however, was fashion's recurring readiness to reveal more and more of the (inevitably

female) body – backless dresses, micro-shorts, 'boob tubes' and crop tops, and the like and – similarly, inspired by the increased body-consciousness of gym culture, **tattoos** and body modification – male youth's preparedness to go topless in even urban settings. ∎

OPPOSITE: *Few people brave the streets with no clothing at all but the acceptance of nudity has influenced our readiness to show off some flesh. Here a woman wears denim cut-offs and a backless top at a festival in Barcelona.*

ABOVE: *That nudity was as much an individual lifestyle choice is perhaps evidenced by this image of a couple of lone naked hippies amid a sea of the conventionally dressed, at the Richmond Pop Festival, London, in 1973.*

Girls will be boys

IDEA № 24
ANDROGYNY

Many iconic figures of the twenty-first century have played with gender expectations through their dress. Artist Frida Kahlo and photographer Lee Miller dressed as men. Film gives the examples of Julie Andrews' character in *Victor Victoria* (1982), Charlotte Rampling in Gestapo uniform in *The Night Porter* (1974), Marilyn Monroe making waves by wearing masculine cowboy garb in *The Misfits* (1961) and, earlier still, during the 1920s and 1930s, the groundbreaking, deliberately outre monocle and top-hat image of Josephine Baker or Marlene Dietrich.

In the 1980s music saw the likes of the Eurythmics' Annie Lennox and Madonna revive the idea of androgyny, as stagewear if not every day, with the twenty-first century seeing actress Tilda Swinton become a new androgyne icon. Androgynous dressing may rarely have been an attempt by women to pass as men – unlike pirates Anne Bonny and Mary Read, or jazz musician Billy Tipton – so much as take on the associations of power and status imbued in male tailoring. In doing so, these women confronted societal expectations that, even into the the twenty-first century, saw some institutions ban women in trousers. But the mainstream effect has been less political, than fashionable: indeed, counter-intuitively perhaps, it has not been about disguising one's sexuality but the wearing of masculine clothes as a way of drawing attention to it, much as Monroe's outfits in *The Misfits*, or Katharine Hepburn's favouring trousers, flat shoes and mannish shirts underlined their femininity.

This is an idea that has been played on in fashion both high – Yves Saint Laurent's re-introduction of the trouser suit for women, or his 'Le Smoking' smoking jacket – and populist. It has encouraged a change, for example, in hairstyles – when once short hair on a woman was indicative of what was then considered sexual deviation (lesbianism), religious devotion (Joan of Arc) or even punishment (women collaborators in France during World War II had their hair cut short as a form of feminine castration), it is now worn in the mould of Mia Farrow's Vidal Sassoon cut for *Rosemary's Baby* (1968). It has also made street style clothing more unisex, particularly for younger generations. Young women are free to share jeans, T-shirts, **hoodies, sportswear** and the like – traditionally male clothing, notably in the urban context – with their male counterparts. Such items have, in fact, redefined a middle ground of clothing that is more asexual – without ownership by either gender.

In stark contrast, although the twentieth century also has examples of male performers the likes of David Bowie, Mick Jagger, Prince and Boy George dabbling in more stereotypically feminine clothing, the effect on the male wardrobe at large has remained negligible. ∎

Practical subversion

IDEA Nº 25
MILITARY UNIFORMS

The comfortable cut and well-engineered functionality of clothes designed for servicemen – especially after World War II, when massive surpluses and high levels of rationing first widely introduced military clothing to the civilian arena – have had consistent and widespread appeal, resonating through civilian life and street culture especially.

Up until the end of the nineteenth century, it was often the cut, colourful dash and impractical high style of a military uniform that was used as an enticement to recruit the shabbily dressed working man. Khaki, or variations on it, became standardized across the majority of national armed forces in the early decades of the twentieth century, although bright colours were still used for dress uniforms. Indeed, khakis became a foundation garment of **preppy** style and a male wardrobe staple to rival denims.

In the later twentieth century, patterns of military camouflage (or DPM, Disruptive Pattern Material) were appropriated by numerous fashion designers – Jean-Charles de Castelbajac and Stephen Sprouse among others – as expressive of urban, inner-city living. NATO's black/grey Arctic camouflage was a style staple for the American rap group Public Enemy, featuring on the cover of their *Yo! Bum Rush the Show* album (1987).

But it has been the more practical twentieth-century designs that have crossed over from military to street cultures, including aviator sunglasses, duffle coats, flight and flak jackets, berets, parkas and T-shirts.

Youth subcultures in particular have seen value in such items being hard-wearing, practical and affordable – hence also readily customized – and have also known how to exploit them for political commentary by recontextualizing, subverting, or in some instances exaggerating, their military origins. When army surplus clothing became widely worn by peace protesters in the 1960s it was genuinely shocking. Since then punks, skinheads, clubbers, skaters, breakers, eco campaigners, rappers, Black Panthers and neo-Nazis alike have all worn it. Arguably the most distinctively military garment to cross over has been the combat trouser. High fashion – led by designers as diverse as Armani, Moschino, Prada and Gaultier – has played with the meanings and moods of military clothing too, as well as drawing inspiration from its clean visual appeal. ∎

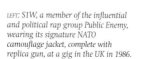
LEFT: S1W, a member of the influential and political rap group Public Enemy, wearing its signature NATO camouflage jacket, complete with replica gun, at a gig in the UK in 1986.

OPPOSITE TOP AND ABOVE: *The cheap, practical and plentiful nature of army surplus clothing has made it part of street style since World War II. But, despite its heyday being the 1960s, Ian Fisk and John Paul's seminal London boutique, I Was Lord Kitchener's Valet looked back further for inspiration to dress uniforms of the late 19th and early 20th centuries. Jimi Hendrix, Eric Clapton and Mick Jagger were among the shop's customers, as was artist Peter Blake, who was consequently inspired for the cover design of the Beatles' Sgt. Pepper's Lonely Hearts Club Band (1967).*

Hotrods and cool kicks

CUSTOMIZATION

'Kids are racing again like I did in the 1950s,' George Barris noted in 2010. 'It was dangerous but it was fun. [A car is] an extension of its owner and, like one's fashion and home, people like to have theirs different to everyone else's. That's what lies at the root of customization: the car as an expression of individuality.'

As the co-founder of Los Angeles Barris Brothers' Custom Shop and the 'King of Kustomizers', as fans have dubbed him, Barris should know. Barris began customizing cars – essentially re-assembling them with different parts, engines, adornments and colourful paintwork – shortly after World War II; by the 1960s he became the first manufacturer of fibreglass bolt-on car accessories; and soon after he was finding work with Hollywood, custom design and building cars for *Batman*, *The Monkees* and *The Munsters*, among others.

Of course, clothes have, since the birth of the teenager, been personalized in order to add a sense of the individual: rockers added chains and artwork to biker jackets,

heavy metal fans wore patches on their denim waistcoats, others have embroidered, appliquéd or stitched – not to mention disassembled – garments to make them more their own, an idea that fashion retailers have pursued with the straight-faced notion of 'pre-customized' garments.

But it is with the vehicle that customization found self-expression – to the point of theatricality – for the street. The writer Tom Wolfe cited Barris as an exemplary of not only the especially young male habit of finding identity through the style of your car, but the need to overhaul it radically to truly make it your own. Barris was, as Wolfe wrote, 'a good example of a kid who grew up in this teenage world of cars, who pursued

the pure flame and its form with such devotion he emerged an artist'. Indeed, by the 1940s, car customization for striking, comic-strip looks had become a cultish underground hobby out of California. Rebuilding cars for speed – so-called 'hot rodding', probably a corruption of 'hot roadster' – proved popular too, given a desert landscape ideal for illegal racing (in fact, the very first hot rod-type cars were built to outrun the police during Prohibition). By 1955 and *Rebel Without a Cause*, in which James Dean's

character almost dies in a 'chickie run' race, custom cars and hotrods had become part of youth culture, as later parodied in 'Greased Lightnin' from the musical *Grease* (1971).

By the time of the musical, more powerful, more luxurious production-line cars had diminished the need to adapt one's wheels for speed (and arguably prompted the new crime of joy-riding). But the desire to give them a personal aesthetic remained and continued to revive periodically: by the 2000s one of MTV's most successful and widely copied TV shows was *Pimp My Ride*, in which young car owners had their vehicle customized for free to reflect their interests and personalities. Customization of fixed wheel bicycles was also popular. ∎

OPPOSITE: *Customizing one's vehicle may have been a bold statement of personal style in the 1950s but it continued to be much more recently too, as with this flame-licked car on Sunset Boulevard in 1992.*

ABOVE: *A customized pair of Nike Air Force One sneakers, in London in 2004.*

Simon Posthuma and Marijke Koger set up the Fool art and fashion collective and opened a shop on London's Baker Street in 1967, specializing in their own take on romantic style. Here, astride a horse, naturally, they model a red velvet cape and brocade Turkish trousers for him, and a silk coat with wide sleeves for her.

Kicking against the corporate

RIGHT: *The Isle of Wight pop festival in 1969, at the height of hippie. In the foreground is Pink Floyd guitarist David Gilmour, his hair suitably long for the times.*

BOTTOM: *Susan Manca has her face painted by William Fuller in Greenwich Village, New York, in 1967. A film casting expert was at hand looking for extras to appear as hippies in Daniel Mann's romantic comedy movie* For Love of Ivy *(1968).*

IDEA № 27
THE HIPPIE

With their long hair, bright colours, flared jeans, sandals and long beaded necklaces, hippies set themselves apart by their often unisex fashion, using the way they dressed as a means of showing an affiliation to the then radical ideas they espoused.

It was perhaps inevitable that the hippie subculture would start in an outsider magnet such as San Francisco, in contrast to the more rigidly business-minded, conservative East Coast. It was in the city's Haight-Ashbury district in the mid-1960s that the early hipsters – from which the 'hippie' name comes – and beatniks came together in a community of shared values, including independence from mainstream society and opposition to war (the Vietnam War in particular). In 1967 the Human Be-In in the city's Golden Gate Park and the West Coast Summer of Love put hippie culture on the national radar; the Woodstock Festival of 1969 – on the East Coast – brought it to international attention.

Hippies spread their ethos of free-living and self-expression through music – rock, blues, folk and psychedelia especially – as well as through literature, film, underground comics, performance arts and, ironically perhaps, commercial art. New, often Eastern, lifestyle practices – such as yoga, meditation, Buddhism, paganism, 'free love', alternative medicines, dietary restrictions such as vegetarianism and veganism – and psychedelic drugs, were all shared experiences.

The hippie look, with its bold patterns and colours – from patchwork to tie-dye – was more than a mere rejection of sobriety and traditionalism, or a reflection of the idealized togetherness of communes and collectives, though both of those were certainly expressed in the loose and free-flowing clothes, from peasant blouses and skirts, to bell-bottom trousers and vests, long hair (for both men and women), beards and bare feet. In being a striking break with the conformism of mainstream youth dress up until the early 1960s, the style aimed to reflect what hippie philosophy stood for: a rejection of the establishment, or 'The Man', the conservative values of World War II and baby boomer generations – and a kick against corporate culture and commercialism.

Consequently, much of the clothing was hand-made or bought from second-hand shops and sometimes customized. Other clothes included garments worn in recognition of ethnic, possibly oppressed, peoples and their philosophies; native clothing from Latin American, Native American and African cultures; and even national dress in some instances. Accessories too, such as headbands, hair ties and beaded necklaces, typically had an ethnic bent. The look – updated, if sometimes verging on cliché – underpinned the style of later subculture groups, including New Age **travellers** and eco-campaigners. ■

Hippie deluxe

BELOW: *Actually shot in 1984, here four models pose to celebrate the 40th anniversary of Barbara Hulanicki's seminal Bohemian store Biba, in 1964. The models all wear original styles, characterized by wide sleeves and flowing swathes of feminine fabric.*

IDEA № 28

BOHEMIANISM

Unlike its hippie counterpart, bohemian style espouses an aesthetic standpoint more than a political one, even if its distant history lies in an interest in poetry, art, literary pursuits and an unconventional lifestyle, such as that embraced by mid- to late nineteenth-century artists and writers such as the Pre-Raphaelites, Charles Baudelaire and Edgar Allen Poe.

Although the original nineteenth-century bohemians took their name from Gypsies – specifically the Romani, who at the time had travelled to western Europe through Bohemia, embodying what was often perceived as a romantic lifestyle of unrooted wandering – most were well-to-do. There was, to some extent, an element of playing at dressing up in the bohemian outlook.

The attitude, if not the style, of being outside mainstream society was echoed some 50 years later in England in the unconventional and artistic mode of life of the Bloomsbury Group and the Slade School of Art set; and another 50 years later in the stylish and decadent look offered by Barbara Hulanicki's influential London store Biba (opened in 1964) and by Laura Ashley (whose first store opened in 1968) in Britain, and in the United States by the hippies.

Following them, bohemianism's place in fashion gave up all pretence of having philosophical leanings, or of being of interest to most men. Bohemianism, or 'boho' as it was abbreviated in the late twentieth century, was generally worn no less by the well-off but became a simple cherry-picking of geographically broad, earthy, free-flowing nomadic looks and colourful national dress styles.

These ranged from Mexican wedding dresses to dirndl skirts, Balkan peasant blouses to 'American Gothic'-style country dresses, worn with cowboy boots or gladiator sandals, grungy outsized knitwear and broad-brimmed hats, and perhaps even with – after the Pre-Raphaelite Effie Gray or Scott McKen-

zie's hippie anthem – flowers in the hair. The look was heavy on accessories, embroidery and layering, bold patterns and overtly feminine fabrics such as silk and chiffon. In the twenty-first century it was a look most widely disseminated through images of off-duty supermodel Kate Moss, through whom a kind of 'boho chic' became a standard look of **festival** goers and the inhabitants of the wealthier parts of metropolitan cities, especially in Europe. ∎

OPPOSITE: *Barbara Hulanicki, founder of Biba, with her husband Stephen Fitz-Simon, in 1975, six years after the first Biba opened in Kensington, west London.*

The chest as canvas

OPPOSITE: T-shirt graphics on display mostly through the early 2000s – retro, political, home-made, comic book and abstract styles are all represented. Top centre is musician Tori Amos, wearing Milton Glaser's famed New York graphic.

BELOW: A British soldier in southern Iraq in 2007 wearing a T-shirt – not an official part of his uniform – expressing a certain dark humour about his job and circumstances.

IDEA № 29
T-SHIRT GRAPHICS

In 1939 the producers of *The Wizard of Oz* recognized the T-shirt's potential as an advertising medium: here, after all, was a blank space that, worn in the right places, would be seen by a lot of people. A basic image from that film consequently became the first example of the T-shirt graphic.

After the war, Thomas Dewey, the Republican candidate in the 1948 American presidential race, launched the campaign T-shirt with his 'Dew it with Dewey' slogan; in 1952 printed T-shirts with the famous 'I Like Ike' slogan appeared in support of Dwight D. Eisenhower. Since then, almost no presidential campaign has been complete without its printed T-shirts.

The idea did not spread, however, until after World War II, when Ed Roth, an ex-GI used to wearing his 'T-type' shirt stencilled with his dog-tag details, launched the first major T-shirt screen-printing business. By the 1950s Tropix Togs in Miami were licensed to print T-shirts with Disney characters – licensing of cartoon and movie imagery and slogans for T-shirts would later become a huge global business. And in 1965 Budweiser – soon followed by the tobacco industry, similarly keen to circumvent advertising restrictions of the time – became the first brand to make use of this inexpensive, mass-market, effective medium; effective because a lot of people were ready to become a human billboard, regardless of the message, for the sake of a free T-shirt.

But it is in the streetwear market since the late 1970s that the T-shirt graphic has been seen more as an artistic medium – provocative, persuasive, witty, entertaining or just good to look at, with a clever slogan or eye-catching image able to resonate long after its wearer has disappeared into the crowd. Such graphics commemorate an event or a place, as with world tour, theme and souvenir T-shirts; protest, as with Alberto Korda's much reproduced image of Che Guevara; or reveal allegiance, whether to a team, a favourite band or a city. Milton Glaser's much-imitated 1976 'I [heart] NY' is perhaps the most famous example of the latter. Some became momentarily cultish: the 'Frankie Says' T-shirts promoting mid-1980s British pop group Frankie Goes to Hollywood, for example, after designer Katharine Hamnett's protest T-shirts. And brands too have run with the idea – the T-shirt is, of course, the perfect place for a large logo. Or, perhaps, a subversive version of one. ∎

Shock and awe in the saddle

IDEA № 30
GREASERS

They called them greasers because they wore their jeans until the dirt and the oil had given them a glossy patina. It was a derogatory term that, adopted and turned around, became a badge of honour. That society should aim to denigrate the greaser was, however, understandable: it feared him. Like the biker taken to extremes, everything about him – from clothing to attitude – denoted self-imposed outsider status.

ABOVE: *As the more outsider and heavy metal/rock-influenced take on rocker, greaser culture has spanned the decades, from the 1950s – as with this youth, displaying his tattoos in New York in 1959 – through to the 1980s and beyond.*

LEFT: *Members of the Bracknell Chopper Club, at a tattoo convention in Dunstable, UK, in 1987.*

The machines and the practical style that bikers often adopted as a hobby – one that many abandoned as their subculture became demonized by the media – the greasers of the late 1960s and early 1970s ramped up and took as a way of life, and certainly as a counterpoint to the prevailing 'love-in' ethos of hippie culture.

To those looking in, the uniform was distinctively rough and grubby, incorporating patched and stained jeans and denim

waistcoats – covered with patches and badges proudly proclaiming membership of a certain biking chapter, a select **heavy metal** band or combative symbols such as swastikas or Iron Crosses – as well as black band T-shirts, and biker jackets heavily customized with studs. Hair was long and lank, often worn with a beard; accessories included wraparound sunglasses, bandanas, chains and metalwork of any kind, and an outré choice of helmet – ex-World War II Wehrmacht standard issue being one such option. Much as a greaser's clothing was a work in progress, evolving both decoratively and through life on the road, so too was his motorcycle, the aesthetic enhancement of which, be it a certain paint job, extra loud pipes or high handle bars, came with the territory.

So determined were greasers to stand outside of societal norms – the regard for Nazi and Satanic symbolism being an example of this, and so too the undisguised carrying of knives, hammers and other hand weapons – that inevitably their look was borrowed by others wishing to effect the same shock factor, if only for the sake of performance. In particular the look was taken up by heavy metal bands, especially in the UK and Europe, as Lemmy, frontman for Motörhead, best demonstrates. ■

The long goatees, wraparound shades, heavily customized leather waistcoats and combat boots single out these three greasers at a rock and blues festival. The waistcoats share the same design, denoting their affiliation, perhaps to a motorcycle club.

Drugs shape fashion

IDEA № 31
PSYCHEDELIA

The popular rise of psychotropic recreational drugs such as LSD during the mid- to late 1960s saw the resulting mental experiences – characteristically vivid, wildly colourful and 'trippy' – transposed on to the visual aesthetic of fine art, commercial art and fashion.

Neon colours, bold geometric or abstract patterns and pattern clashes, and a flamboyance in detail – outsized cuffs, ruffles and trimmings – together with 'ethnic' styles such as kaftans, marked a distinct break with the rigorous, pared-down modernism of the mods, dominant until the middle of the decade.

After this mid-point a more theatrical style of dressing up shaped the psychedelic style: the bold patterns exaggerated through bell-bottom or flared-sleeve silhouettes, for instance. Influential fashion hotspots included Carnaby Street, one of the centres of 'Swinging London', and stores such as John Pearse, Sheila Cohen and Nigel Waymouth's Granny Takes a Trip (opened in 1965) on King's Road. Work by such designers as Thea Porter, Zandra Rhodes, Jean Muir and Ossie Clark helped give the psychedelic look a credibility among fashion followers. Costumiers Paul Reeves and Pete Sutch created one-off outfits for the likes of Jimi Hendrix and Jimmy Page that led to more commercial versions – made from Indian bed covers – sold through antiques markets, Mick Jagger and George Harrison being among the customers.

But psychedelic fashion was also part of a wider societal shift. The burgeoning drug scene that shaped the look was just one facet of a growing counterculture during the period. It embodied a disillusionment with Western consumerism and a resultant turning to the East, with its supposed mysticism, or a readiness to drop out of mainstream society. In popular culture the feeling was expressed by such albums as the Beatles' *Sgt. Pepper's Lonely Hearts Club Band* (1967), movies including *Easy Rider* (1969) and events such as the 1967 Summer of Love on America's West Coast. In fashion, it translated into a more random, home-made approach to the way one dressed. ∎

'Psychedelic fashion was also part
of a wider societal shift.'

Hasta la victoria siempre!

IDEA Nº 32
MILITANT CHIC

When Alberto Korda photographed the Cuban revolutionary Che Guevara in his signature black beret in 1960, he could not have known that the image would become a symbol to youth of empowerment and rebellion of almost mythic proportions – and more, would also effectively become a brand.

According to the Victoria and Albert Museum in London, Korda's photograph – for which he received not a cent in royalties – has been reproduced more than any other in history. The shot would become one of the most iconic T-shirt graphics ever, and illustrates the way in which the iconography of militancy is taken up by fashion.

The radicalism of the freedom fighter (or terrorist, depending on where one is standing) has been reflected in popular culture and clothing since the mid-1960s, when the revolutionary left-wing Black Power ideology of the Black Panthers attained a countercultural cool. Its uniform – decided on by leading Black Panther activists Huey and Melvin Newton – comprised black trousers, black berets, blue shirts and black leather jackets (black and leather both similarly, paradoxically, having been style tropes favoured by extreme right-wing organizations). The Black Panther look was admired and sometimes mimicked by rich American socialites drawn to extreme politics and identified by writer Tom Wolfe as being in thrall to 'radical chic', and the look was later echoed in the style of politicized rap acts such as Public Enemy.

The keffiyeh, black-and-white scarf or head-wrap, traditionally worn by Palestinian men became a symbol of Palestinian nationalism from the 1930s onwards, and especially so in the 1960s when it became the trademark headgear of Yasser Arafat; the keffiyeh was adopted by fashion followers from the 1980s onwards, usually with no intentional political connotations, although that did not prevent American fashion retailer Urban Outfitters from having to withdraw its coloured keffiyehs and issue an apology following complaints.

Fashion also appropriated the imagery of the Baader-Meinhof Gang, which terrorized West Germany from 1967 to 1977: some decades after the death or imprisonment of

its principal members, the iconography associated with group – notably the logo of the Red Army Faction (as the Gang was later known) – was found on T-shirts and inspiring 'Prada-Meinhof' fashion shoots of the kind controversially run by *Der Spiegel*. ∎

HERE AND OPPOSITE: *Party goers at London's Notting Hill Carnival, a part of the city with a large West Indian, Caribbean and Rasta community. Both men wear the colours of the Ethiopian flag – red, green and yellow.*

Style as an expression of belief

IDEA № 33
RASTA

Few subcultures are so distinctively identified by a hairstyle. But dreadlocks are central to the Rastafari faith. As in the biblical story of Samson, there is a belief that strength – more spiritual than physical – lies in them, while their easy maintenance perhaps expresses a rejection of the vanity suggested by modern haircare products.

Dreadlocks also have links to slavery – Jamaican Rastafari first adopted dreads in the 1930s, when the Rastafari movement began, as a symbolic reminder of their ancestors being in chains.

The Rasta look has been much emulated, especially following the global fame of reggae star Bob Marley from the 1970s onwards; in the following decade (sometimes artificial) dreads were even worn by white people, in part for fashion, in part by 'eco-warrior' environmentalists as a way of expressing a peace-loving ethos, perhaps one of being more in tune with the natural world rather than the industrial and commercial one – ideas that are also central to the Rastafari movement.

Rastafari worship the Ethiopian emperor Haile Selassie I (ruled 1930–74), seeing him as a messiah figure and believing that his coronation was the first prophesied step in a black 'Zion', overcoming the imposed dominance of a white 'Babylon' in Africa. To Rastas themselves, much of what is worn has a deeper significance: it is style as an expression of a shared belief. The dominant colours – green, red, gold – which feature on T-shirts, scarves, badges and the 'tam', or knitted cap, are those of the Ethiopian flag; black also often features, symbolizing Africa. Loose clothing in natural fibres is preferred – in harmony with the natural world. Women wear traditional African headdresses, in a nod to their spiritual homeland. And during the 1970s, even the adoption of combat fatigues as part of the look was to express support for Cuban revolutionaries fighting in Angola.

Such subtleties, however, are likely to be lost on the student wearing a T-shirt bearing a marijuana leaf in Ethiopian colours or the catwalk collections' periodic references to 'reggae style'. ∎

ABOVE: *At the Shashemene Rasta community in Ethiopia in 1964, Gladstone Robinson, one of the first Rasta men to emigrate from the US to Rasta's spiritual home, sits with his youngest daughter. Above him hangs a portrait of Haile Selassie, the subject of Rasta worship.*

Proud to be proletarian

IDEA № 34
SKINHEAD

Perhaps no style movement has been so widely misunderstood as the skinheads. Their strong image, defined by heavy boots and close-cropped hair, made the cult a byword for the extreme right-wing politics and racism that would hijack it. The origins of the original skinhead could hardly have been further away.

Skinhead – the word itself did not enter parlance until 1969, the style's adherents being dubbed cropheads, lemons and boiled eggs before – was a late 1960s assertion of smart dress of British inner-city, working-class origins (and so, ironically, far more likely to be left-leaning politically). Often described as the remnants of mod – sharing mod's love of scooters, for example, and frequently referred to as 'hard mods' – skinheads sought a streamlined, simple, almost blunt style of dress that stood for rejection of the flowery, fanciful, long-haired psychedelic style of the period.

The clothes were accessible, affordable and proletarian, with every intention of reflecting group solidarity rather than individuality, but were worn with exacting precision. By night that meant a mohair suit (in fact, skinheads were initially referred to as 'suits'), polished brogues and Crombie-style coat; by day, more distinctively, Harrington jacket, button-down or polo shirt, braces and army fatigues or denims rolled up to show decidedly workman-like (sometimes steel-capped) and always highly polished boots, later characteristically Dr. Martens. Far from being scruffy, this was a look that was obsessively considered and all the more so for being an expression of intense class pride – like Teddy boy before, skinhead was a culture that genuinely came up from the street, attracting no middle-class following. This was perhaps underscored by skinheads, for all their love of reggae and ska music, being essentially a tribe channelled by football, much as **casuals** were a decade later.

While the original skinheads had moved away from the look by the early 1970s – increased association with football violence meant that skinhead style attracted constant negative attention, from the police especially – as a style and a culture skinhead would continue to resonate over subsequent decades, attracting a dedicated following in pockets internationally in a way that no other British style subculture has done. ∎

Skinheads in the more exaggerated uniform of the revivalist period – MA1 flight jacket, cropped jeans and higher-lacing boots, with contrasting laces – expressing the anti-social tendencies of the period too.

Style as racial harmony

IDEA № 35
TWO TONE

Two Tone was a record label before it was a style, but the style and the music were irrevocably intertwined. Founded in Coventry, UK, in 1979 by Jerry Dammers of the Specials, with a deliberate multiracial angle, it aimed to create a company through which British ska could be developed. This was a distinct evolution of the ska sound that had originated in Jamaica in the 1950s and 1960s, brought to Britain chiefly through immigration from the West Indies.

ABOVE: *Two young Two Tone/ska fans in its British spiritual home, Coventry in 1980 – their style characterized by the narrow-brimmed hat and the chequerboard badges.*

Never a fully evolved style, the Two Tone look was a mix of mod and skinhead influences, crossed with that of the rude boys – the Jamaican street toughs-cum-enforcers of the Caribbean island's criminal underworld, admired for their style. The rude-boy look amounted to colourful trilby, pork-pie or so-called 'stingy brim' hat, skinny ties, colourful shirts and dark suits, worn with the trouser legs some 15 centimetres (6 inches) shorter than normal in order to show off socks and loafers or boots. When Jamaican ska star Desmond Dekker toured the UK and was given a suit to wear by his agency, he insisted on the trousers being shortened before he would wear them.

In the UK, Two Tone and its influential bands – including the Selecter, the Beat, the Bodysnatchers and, briefly, Madness – wore the look, but in black and white. This, in part, was an expression of Two Tone's politics: just as its music was a means of promoting progressive multiracialism and racial unity, so these beliefs were reflected in the black-and-white dress, a style that also echoed the minimalist style of French New Wave cinema. Two Tone fans – called rude boys and rude girls in the UK – dressed snappily in button-down shirts, straight-leg (and slightly short) trousers, white socks and loafers or brogues for boys, and ski pants or miniskirts (often in black-and-white panels or checks) and tights for girls; accessories included trilbies, Ray-Ban Wayfarers or wrap-around shades, and narrow red, black or white braces (one way in which the look blurred with skinhead).

Although the heyday of the Two Tone record label lasted only 18 months, the style, and its multiracial message, was made more widely popular by the label's consistent graphic imagery, directed by Dammers and designed by David Storey of parent record company Chrysalis. This focused on a Pop art-style black-and-white chequerboard pattern and a graphic character nicknamed Walt Jabsco, the archetype of the rude boy, hands in pockets and complete with his Ray-Bans. Ironically, given Two Tone's efforts – both as a record label and as a style – to promote racial harmony at a time of ongoing racial tension in the UK, the press widely misrepresented Two Tone as the music beloved by racist thugs. ∎

RIGHT: *The Selector, shot in 1980, with their frontwoman Pauline Black, whose androgynous, if still more feminine take on Two Tone, saw her attain style icon status during the period.*

BELOW: *The Specials, the definitive band of Two Tone, at Hurrah's in New York in 1980. Left and eating pizza is the pioneer of Two Tone – musically, stylistically, graphically – Jerry Dammers. Behind him is a taciturn Terry Hall, who would bring the slow demise of Two Tone's high times by leaving the band (and the style) to form Fun Boy Three.*

Retro as lifestyle

REVIVALISM

There is, as the saying goes, nothing new in fashion. It feeds on the past, its ideas and moods, reinventing them, updating them, sometimes merely reproducing them. Style subcultures play a part in this, leaving their imprint on fashion to be assessed and reassessed over decades. But then there is revivalism – when a major subculture of the past goes mainstream and is adopted as a lifestyle rather than a one-season fad, albeit in an aesthetically more concentrated form.

ABOVE: *Two mods, more modish than most Mods of the 1960s – and this is in the early 2000s, UK.*

OPPOSITE: *Mods they may be, but these two – Paula and Mark – are of the 2007 school, not that of the 1960s or 1970s.*

BELOW: *If the Teddy boy's true time was the post-war austerity years of the 1950s, then perhaps those of the 1970s, as here in 1976, were inevitably more style over substance. Elements of the revival look –contrast suit collars, as here, for example – would not have been recognizably 'Ted' the first time around.*

The Teddy boy movement of the mid- to late 1950s underwent a revival in the 1970s, much as the mod subculture of the early to mid-1960s did in the late 1970s and early 1980s – and rarely to the approval of those who were part of the respective cultures the first time around. The Teddy boy historian John van Rheede Toas has described the 1970s incarnation, epitomized by such bands as Showaddywaddy and Mud, all pastel-coloured Ted suits, Lurex, boot-lace ties and extra-high brothel creepers, as an 'abomination'. The revival, as is often the case, picked up certain style cues and exaggerated them, sometimes almost to the point of parody, even if the homage was well-meaning.

The same might be said of the second wave of mod, inspired by the release of the movie *Quadrophenia* in 1979: while not as stylistically extreme as the Ted revival, it did reduce the breadth and creativity of original mod style to stylistic tropes – the parka, skinny Italian suits, over-customized scooters, graphics such as the RAF roundel – with such a focus that it

realigned the meaning of the first-wave subculture in the public imagination. Indeed, it patently looked back while the original mod(ernist)s looked only forward. Sometimes such a process destroys the intent of the first wave: in the mid- to late 1960s skinhead grew out of homegrown British working-class community spirit and a love of both ska and football; its revivalist version, a decade later, was almost entirely co-opted by extreme right-wing politics.

Perhaps what distinguishes the later incarnations of a style subculture from its first wave is less the lack of subtlety that pervades the style the second time around so much as its lack of innocence. An original style subculture starts from the position of self-creation rather than imitation – with, often, a genuine shock factor or a revolutionary change to fashion that in revivals goes unappreciated. It is a shared passion leading to an original style rather than an in-crowd looking to the past. ■

Super-fly style takes off

IDEA № 37
FUNK

'I know Shaft's a fantasy person,' Richard Roundtree said in an interview in 1972. 'But the image the kids see of him on the screen is of a black man who is for once a winner. There are very few black people to my knowledge who have been idolized the way John Shaft has. Kids are running around in black leather jackets and are swaggering – that whole Shaft number, man.'

Shaft was the film, released the previous year, about a super-hip black detective of the same name, played by Roundtree, an ex-model. It spawned a number of so-called 'blaxploitation' films (a controversial genre considered by some as positive for black culture, by others as perpetuating stereotypes) offering a different black male image, which in turn cemented the idea of a specifically black style aesthetic: sexual – fitted in all the right places, flared in others to exaggerate the tightness elsewhere – and dark, in leather jacket as in turtleneck, the whole capped with the era's symbol of emergent black power, an Afro hairstyle. 'This dude is bad, and he isn't just fly – he's super fly,' proclaimed the trailer for *Super Fly* (1972).

This was one of the earliest blaxploitation films to use a fashion designer, in this case Nate Adams, for the costumes, and 'super fly' became a slang term of approval for anyone dressed with a certain self-confidence and sense of showmanship, be they film character, funk musician or hustler. The films similarly, though less so, helped define black women's style, with the likes of Pam Grier in *Foxy Brown* (1974) stressing the bold and the sexual. Brown is described as 'a whole lot of woman'.

It was all, in the parlance of the time, 'funky' – from 'funk', a street term applied to the late 1960s and 1970s black style of music, food, arts and fashion – and arguably the first time that aspirant pop culture had been

shaped by a style of black origin, even if it was one ostensibly borrowed from the look of black ghetto hustlers of the period, who wore their wealth (and, by inference at the time, their sexual potency) on their backs. The parody of pimp style may since have become the definition in the public imagination – loud, excessive, big broad-brimmed hats, all exotic skins and fur trim, the look adopted for the stage by funk musicians such as Bootsy Collins and George Clinton – but then its more true-to-life, subtly stylish incarnation visually represented the black urban counterculture. If the white counterculture dressed down against conservatism, the black counterculture dressed up, or even out-dressed it. ∎

Photographer Allan Tannenbaum's celebrated shot of James Brown in short-sleeved, kick-flared leisure suit, doing one of his trademark stage jumps on Broadway in New York, 1979.

'Any trope for an outsider nature would become part of the heavy metal style... not just a love of black...'

The anti-metrosexual

IDEA № 38
HEAVY METAL

The machismo of heavy metal might seem counter to the idea that its look is highly theatrical, but when Rob Halford of British heavy metal band Judas Priest first went on stage in 1978 dressed in head-to-toe black leather, it was more than merely a nod to the rockers or to Gene Vincent. This was costume – inspired, Halford would say, by the leather subculture of bondage.

Glam metal, just one of heavy metal's many subsets, had already explored such stage-craft in its own boldly excessive way, making animal prints, snakeskin, skintight trousers and big, backcombed hair all part of a colourful ensemble – more Kiss than Black Sabbath, with the likes of Night Ranger and Mötley Crüe drawing on 1970s glam, all theatrical make-up, backcombed hair, headbands and colourful spandex, all of which would make it especially appealing to the early music video/MTV couture of the 1980s. But classic heavy metal style was the more honest, down-and-dirty

take – and certainly less televisual or family-friendly for that.

Any trope of an outsider nature would become part of the heavy metal style (the term 'heavy metal' was derived from the phrase 'heavy metal thunder' from Steppenwolf's late 1960s hit 'Born To Be Wild'): not just a love of black but of metal studs, from bondage and biker culture; badges, also from biking; denim or leather vests and big hats, from American western style; sometimes dark make-up, from glam rock and goth; and plenty of big jewellery. Accessories were chosen in part for their shock value

(shock of course being one trope of rock and roll), from religious and Satanic iconography, as well as that of Saxon, Viking and Celtic history, through to Nazi militaria.

This was all wrapped around a band T-shirt and, in an unlikely fusion with hippie style, a general dishevelment: long, seemingly unwashed hair, beards, holed and torn clothing. The emphasis of heavy metal style was on group unity through a shared passion and a seeming back-to-basics lack of concern about appearance; a lack of concern about very much at all, in fact, aside from pleasure in the here and now. ∎

The death of subculture

BELOW AND OPPOSITE: *The real thing and the fashion version. From the Beatles in 1963 through to Culture Club in the 1980s, via the likes of David Bowie, Marc Bolan and Two Tone, influential performers (for their look as much as their music) have quickly been copied by the fashion industry, especially by mail order. 'Send [your cheque] now and get with it!' as the small ad offering a 'Beatle-style' jacket promises. Arguably by the 1990s, with the advent of fast fashion, and the proliferation of multimedia, multichannel culture, few acts could command such attention, and it became perhaps undesirable to dress like them, rather than as trends dictated.*

IDEA Nº 39
COMMERCIALIZATION

The problem with style subcultures, noted Dick Hebdige, author of the seminal *Subculture: The Meaning of Style*, is that inevitably most suffer from exposure: the underground goes overground. He cited mod as a case in point: even when mod was still in its heyday, interest in it among mods began to wane as soon as the pioneering British pop music TV programme *Ready Steady Go!* not only focused on mod-favoured music but borrowed mod iconography for its set.

Commerce too plays a part as subcultural ways of dress are repackaged by fashion companies for a mass audience, often in a diluted, more accessible form. The music press, generally preceding the style press, would not only cover the style elements of the bands that formed the latest music movements – music being the foundation of many style subcultures – but would soon be running classified ads encouraging those outside them to get the look. 'For Boys & Girls – Latest Fashions – Lowest Prices' proclaimed one such advertisement from the 1970s, offering 'mod trousers', 'ska jackets with one button and matching baggy ska trousers' and even 'Bowie jacket (as David Live LP)' and 'satin Bowie ties'.

The consequence was that, in order to maintain the group identity and exclusivity that in part made them appealing in the first place, subcultures either had to constantly reinvent themselves or, what was more likely, face a short lifespan before being absorbed by the mainstream. Indeed, some of the more seminal style subcultures lasted only a matter of months. Some subcultures, in particular those espousing as much an ideology as a style, have considered commercialization as directly at odds with their philosophy: both **punk**'s and hip hop's rejection of conformity suffered in going overground.

More recent developments in media only exacerbated the problem; it has been argued that the internet, and the speed with which it disseminates coverage of subcultures that previously would have remained undiscovered for some time, means that style subcultures can no longer take root, and exert an influence, as they did until the early 1990s. New style subcultures now are short-lived and predominantly an adjunct to fashion trends, rather than their aesthetic being part of a more complete lifestyle. ∎

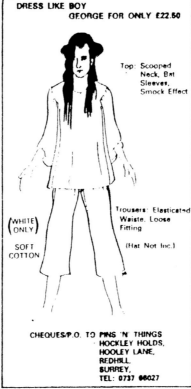

DRESS LIKE BOY
GEORGE FOR ONLY £22.50

Top: Scooped Neck, Bat Sleeves, Smock Effect

(WHITE ONLY)

SOFT COTTON

Trousers: Elasticated Waist, Loose Fitting

(Hat Not Inc.)

CHEQUES/P.O. TO PINS 'N' THINGS
HOCKLEY HOLDS,
HOOLEY LANE,
REDHILL,
SURREY,
TEL: 0737 66027

We're all crazy now

IDEA Nº 40
GLAM

When glam erupted on to the British music and fashion scenes in the early 1970s (and later, as glam metal, in the United States), it was widely dismissed as a joke. While the cool modernism of the early 1960s had morphed into a free-flowing and flowery psychedelia that reached its pinnacle at the 'peace and music' exposition of Woodstock in 1969, glam's new excesses were considered cartoonish.

The guitar-driven music was rambunctious and rollicking, against, for example, the more straight-faced offering of prog rock or the machismo of heavy metal. And the clothing, with its emphasis on the spectacular and overtly theatrical – at times pantomimic – introduced not only to performance but to the wider fashion world a new emphasis on self-expression and fun. As skinhead-turned-glam band Slade had it, 'Mama, weer all crazee now'.

Glitter, sequins, costume jewellery, batwing-sleeved shirts , skintight satin trousers, shiny space-age metallic fabrics, super-sized flares, sci-fi jumpsuits, towering knee-high platform boots (often by shoe designer Terry de Havilland), decorative make-up and big, wildly coloured hair – and that was just the men – all became typical aspects of dress. At least, they did for such artists as the Sweet, David Bowie (as Ziggy Stardust), Gary Glitter, Wizzard, Suzi Quatro, Roxy Music and T. Rex. The moment when T. Rex's frontman Marc Bolan wore glitter under his eyes for a *Top of the Pops* TV performance in 1971 is frequently cited as the genesis of glam.

As Bowie put it of Ziggy Stardust, these were clothes for 'a character who looks like he's landed from Mars'. More subtle, socially acceptable touches were quickly adopted by the fashion mainstream until around 1975, when glam went into decline and equally brash punk arose (although in Japan, glam saw echoes in the flamboyant pop/rock style of Visual Kai from the early 1980s). In that half-decade period, however, glam's dressing-up-box, anything-goes aesthetic revolutionized ideas of what was acceptable clothing off-stage. Particularly for men, a new **androgyny**, if not femininity, was possible, in part because it always came packaged with the intriguingly stark contrast of driving, aggressive, rock-inspired music. Stylistically, glam would reverberate through 1980s' New Romanticism and, later, such acts as Lady Gaga. ∎

The unbuyable must-have

IDEA № 41

COOL

The old saying goes that if you think you're cool, you almost certainly are not. But as ineffable as 'cool' is as a quality – and the French imply this very fact in calling it 'je ne sais quoi' – it has become a defining idea of street style, being above it, but also shaping its aspirations.

Indeed, the word has entered the international lexicon precisely because to be cool, or to be perceived as cool is, in superficial terms, the ultimate accolade. It puts one closer to such icons of cool as James Dean (assisted as many are by untimely death), Bob Dylan or Steve McQueen, Marlene Dietrich, Patti Smith or Charlotte Gainsbourg.

Historic figures could be cool too: even in 1528 the Italian courtier Baldassare Castiglioni was calling the cool of the time 'sprezzatura', a façade of effortless nonchalance that modern Italian culture defines in part as 'la bella figura'. Cool was, as Castiglioni put it then, the 'universal rule in all human affairs'. Cool was also seen as a stance of inner defiance for nineteenth-century black African slaves, later feeding into blues and jazz.

Certainly it is partly about individualistic style, partly about sex appeal, but perhaps above all it is about maintaining a genuine disregard for what anyone else thinks – especially about whether anyone else thinks you are cool. It is their cool that has made the aforementioned figures role models, in fashion but also in manner. Academics Dick Pountain and David Robins define cool as 'a permanent state of private rebellion. Permanent because cool is not just some "phase that you go through" but rather something that if once attained remains for life; private because cool is a stance of individual defiance, which does not announce itself in strident slogans but conceals its rebellion behind a mask of ironic passivity.'

Cool can also be applied to a thing as much as to a person, and cool is, like fashion, a reflection of the times: what one generation ranks as cool – as authentic, as original, as 'hip' or whatever it chooses to call it – the next will not. It is what fashion brands try to define and package, not always successfully – perhaps straying into clichés of cool, archetypically those permanent sunglasses – to such an extent that it has been suggested that cool has become simply another aspect of commerce. ∎

ABOVE: *French actress Charlotte Gainsbourg, posing for a portrait shot in Paris. Her slouchy trousers and belted mac – something of a quirky signature – helped give her that cool 'je ne sais quoi'.*

OPPOSITE: *Actor James Dean (1931–1955), perhaps the very embodiment of male cool in the 20th century.*

Otherworld glamour

IDEA Nº 42
DISCO

During the late 1960s and early 1970s, the advent of the discothèque, and with it disco music – a softer, more upbeat, Latin- or funk-inspired alternative to the dominant rock of the period – formalized not only the idea of dancing on one's own, but also the idea of a certain new peacockery in dress.

ABOVE: *John Travolta's turn as Tony Manero in* Saturday Night Fever *– in a white three-piece suit – helped define the look of disco for subsequent generations. The film's original soundtrack, by the Bee Gees, similarly helped define the disco sound.*

BELOW: *It may be Halloween but only the theatricality and glamour of disco – and especially that at New York's pioneering club Studio 54 – necessitated turning up for a night out on a white horse.*

OPPOSITE: *Excess, dressing up and revelry at Studio 54. At certain points in the evening, the club's light poles would descend from the ceiling on to the dance floor, casting everything in red light.*

Dressing for the disco – a bubble of glamour in contrast to the grey and economically uncertain real world outside – was about dressing up. The iconic image of John Travolta's Tony Manero in *Saturday Night Fever* (1977) in his white three-piece leisure suit (a suit he could ill afford, but one essential for dance-floor presence) was close to the truth.

Indeed, the sexualized atmosphere of the disco – taken to extremes in supposed dens of iniquity such as New York's famed Studio 54 – ushered in what was sometimes referred to specifically as 'disco-wear'. Notably for women this included the likes of stretchy, fitted spandex tops, hot pants and sheer fabrics, to highlight the bodily form, as well as catsuits and 'disco pants', often in colours and shiny synthetic fabrics that caught the disco lights as a glitter-ball did. Hipster jeans and bell bottoms, while part of 1970s fashion at large, were often favoured by men precisely because they exaggerated movement and emphasized the groin as they moved. Shirts would be worn open several buttons down. Jewellery was abundant on both men and women. As Sister Sledge had it in their song 'He's the Greatest Dancer' (1979), the disco was a showground for 'Halston, Gucci, Fiorucci'.

This superficiality – disco's emphasis as much on fashion as music – and hedonism was arguably at the root of the disco back-lash by the end of the decade, when such mantras as 'disco sucks' became common-place and the genre and the places alike were castigated by some for their lack of authenticity. After the supposed depth of hippie, and against the aggression of punk, disco seemed all too frothy and frivolous. ■

Anarchy in the wardrobe

IDEA № 43
PUNK

If youth is often characterized as embodying disaffection with the status quo, then perhaps no single subculture has more stridently captured the spirit of wild rebellion than punk. As the Sex Pistols put it: 'No future.' Those two words would become a nihilistic manifesto for the movement, although 'no past' may have been more accurate, since punk was born of an ideology that disavowed predecessors and the mainstream, and aimed at the new, self-created and often shocking.

In style terms, punk was the progenitor of DIY fashion as a means of self-expression rather than necessity. The DIY approach ran through all things punk. It did not matter if you knew only three chords – that was enough to start a band; self-expression flourished as much in punk's often iconographic and satirical graphic design and in its 'zines' and other literature as it did in the music's typically low-fi, repetitive and aggressive bursts of thrashy guitar.

For the great mass of punks, it applied most clearly to home-made and home-designed fashion – clothes were ripped up and reassembled, references from fashion history were cherry-picked and juxtaposed in new looks. Vivienne Westwood and Malcolm McLaren led the way in 1971 with designs for their shop Let It Rock (renamed Sex in 1974) on London's King's Road, but they were part of a bigger scene.

Indeed, punk was as much a youth-defined and -defining philosophical and artistic movement as a combative form of music or fashion. Combative in fashion it certainly was though: while the picture postcard version of the London punk hardly existed during punk's heyday, the T-shirts worn by the Sex Pistol's Johnny Rotten and Sid Vicious at their first gig at London's 100 Club, espoused the attitude: the former's sported an image from a gay porn magazine, the latter one of a pile of corpses in Auschwitz. Punk, as McLaren put it, was 'a look that you could create for yourself. If you couldn't afford to buy a tailor-made vinyl outfit, you could just grab a bin liner and stick it over your head and still be groovy.' It was, he said, 'the new rebel outlaw look'.

While punk has been caricatured as a mohican, a safety pin, a snarl, bondage trousers, bleach-splashed T-shirt, leather/PVC drainpipes or rubber skirt, self-imposed alienation and plenty of bad guitar-playing, its anti-establishment standpoint provided young people of the 1970s, chiefly in Britain

and the United States, with a progressive political ideology that encouraged them to question entrenched attitudes in society such as capitalism, racism, sexism and nationalism.

Authenticity, in fact – of action, of attitude, of spirit – became punk's underpinning. And with much of society of the 1970s and early 1980s opposed to everything you were and all you appeared to represent, authenticity was required to stay the course. Staying true to the cause of punk as an

all-embracing lifestyle, rather than regarding it as a passing fashion or fad, defined those deep in it, which in part explains why punk remains an aesthetic and an outlook several decades on. ∎

OPPOSITE: *John Lydon, frontman for seminal British punk band the Sex Pistols, with Malcolm McLaren, the band's manager and so-called Svengali figure. Certainly it was largely McLaren's idea to manage a band precisely as a means of selling the clothes designed by him and his then fledgling fashion designer partner Vivienne Westwood.*

ABOVE: *The punk archetype – and stuff of London tourist postcards – giving the V-sign to a policeman, albeit only when his back is turned, in 1983.*

Badges of skill

RIGHT: *Northern soul style was often shaped by the acrobatics of the dance moves – fitted vests and baggy trousers allowed ease of movement.*

BELOW: *Northern soul, as a sound and a style, lasted among devotees well beyond its heyday. Here, two northern soulies at an all-nighter in Salford, northern England, in the late 1990s pose with their badges, each commemorating their attendance at a northern soul event of note.*

IDEA Nº 44
NORTHERN SOUL

Towards the end of the 1970s, *Billboard* magazine, the US music industry bible, voted Wigan Casino as the world's best disco, ahead even of New York's legendary Studio 54. High praise for an obscure venue in Britain's Northwest – but it was there, along with a handful of other venues, that so-called northern soul was born, a largely underground movement comprising the fanatical·followers of obscure 1960s black soul music.

The movement began in the late 1960s and spread through Manchester, Stoke, Blackpool and other northern cities until the closure of Wigan Casino in 1981. Along with a love of the music produced by labels such as Motown, Stax and Atlantic but at the time deemed insufficiently commercial for release, came not only a (sometimes illicit) trade in rare vinyl, which attracted record prices, but a form of acrobatic dancing involving spins, flips, splits and kicks, which prefigured **breaking** in the United States. And for this was required a style of clothing that gave freedom of movement but also allowed its wearer to cope with the heat in often packed and poorly ventilated venues.

Heavy, leather-soled brogues were worn as they offered the best level of 'slide' on sometimes rudimentary dance floors (dancers would sometimes sprinkle talc on the floor to help them make their dance moves). Favoured were wide, Oxford bag-style trousers, some up to 80 centimetres (32 inches) wide, sometimes with multiple pockets on the rear or extravagant waist-bands. Into these might be tucked a beer towel, with which to wipe away perspiration. The trousers would be worn either with a loose American-style bowling shirt or, more typically, a vest or racer-back singlet. And on to this were sewn cloth badges, or patches, denoting membership of a specific northern

soul appreciation club or attendance at a particular event or club night.

The look – although soon considered clichéd by northern soul aficionados – was more than a fashion, since it was not worn outside of the all-night dance meetings and often was decidedly not in keeping with mainstream style of the time. And it expressed more than an allegiance to the music. Indeed, although many northern soulies would have the badges – putting them, for example, on their sports holdalls, in which they carried a change of clothes – in a sense one had to earn the right to wear them: through one's abilities on the dance floor. ■

Northern soul dancers at the Mousetrap Weekender in London in 2010. The dancer on the right wears a Ben Sherman shirt, a northern soul favourite.

Classless comfort

IDEA № 45
SPORTSWEAR AS STREETWEAR

Specialist clothing for sports activities has influenced mainstream fashion since the 1920s. Golf sweaters and tennis shirts, hunting tweeds and ski wear, attire for riding and cycling all made the transition from their original purpose with the growing appeal of the way they looked – or, more often, felt, especially following the revolution in synthetic fibres during the 1950s.

But it was not until the late 1970s and early 1980s, initially in the US but soon across western Europe, that sportswear (in the sense of clothing designed for sport) became less an influence on fashion than a youth street fashion in its own right. This was less about functionality and ease, as important as those factors were, than the rising kudos of sports brands, their mass-market accessibility compared with the exclusivity of designer brands at the time, and their efforts

to tap into fashion markets. Sport was the catwalk for the everyman.

Indeed, many brands pursued this youth market while denying that fashion played a huge part in their success; they were, they claimed, all about professional sports performance and just happened to appeal to young consumers. Yet the likes of Adidas, Champion and Le Coq Sportif meanwhile embraced their early association with hip hop, while Nike's multi-million dollar

marketing programmes helped make sports stars into fashion leaders, most notably following its 1984 design and endorsement deal with superstar basketball player Michael Jordan.

Key items in the sports locker – T-shirts, sweatshirts, sweatpants, hoodies, **sneakers**, as well as accessories such as baseball caps – soon became staples of streetwear, sparking designs by new, dedicated streetwear companies. Sport even shaped the dominant aesthetic of early streetwear – boldly

coloured, graphic-heavy – and the way in which early streetwear was worn. Efforts in the United States by, for example, the National Football League and National Basketball League to sell merchandise saw their clothing worn on the street in the sizes made for their professional players: outsize became a streetwear standard.

Ironically perhaps, by the late 1980s and early 1990s sportswear was starting to distance itself from its democratic beginnings and ape the exclusivity of the designer clothing with which it had had such a strong contrast: limited editions, special collaborations and – through style movements like casual in the UK – the pursuit of ever more esoteric or hard-to-find sportswear came to introduce an element of sartorial one-upmanship. ∎

ABOVE: *UK rapper Tinchy Stryder and Ruff Sqwad, in 2005, showing a preference for American-style sportswear despite the London setting.*

OPPOSITE: *Three teenage girls in Chicago, USA, in 1997, their clothing including both official NFL merchandise, and what looks to be counterfeit Ralph Lauren Polo – the heavily branded nature of sportswear making it a primary target for counterfeiters.*

Jane Fonda, Queen of Aerobics: her videos were the driving force behind the international phenomenon aerobics became in the 1980s.

Fashion to sweat in

RIGHT: Aerobics crept out of the exercise studio and into mainstream style, most notably with the taking up of leg warmers, even if other parts of the body were left exposed to the elements.

BELOW: Angie Best, world record keep-fit workout fundraiser for the British 1984 Olympic Games appeal, takes a crowd of Lycra, head-band, leotard and leg-warmer-clad followers through a routine at a football ground in London in 1984.

IDEA Nº 46
AEROBICS STYLE

The 1980s' new interest in health and fitness saw exercise reconsidered as an activity in which everyone should participate, and do so beyond the traditional realms of school gym and sports field. The exercise class rapidly became the accessible means of enjoying a routine of organized high-energy movement under expert tuition; despite being coined in 1968, 'aerobics' became the lifestyle buzzword.

Usually performed to music, aerobics required particular clothes, including fitted leotards, unitards, sweatbands, leg warmers and cropped crossover cardigans (the latter two items being borrowed from ballet attire). Since aerobics was targeted mostly at women – it was the first time the public gym was anything other than a male preserve – style remained important. But this was style you could sweat in.

The clothing borrowed not only its often high-tech materials from the professional outdoors and sports performance arena – for example, spandex/Lycra was used for tights, leotards and figure-hugging tops – but also its colour palette of garish brights and neon detailing: yellow, purple and electric blue were especially popular. The look quickly became an influence on mainstream fashion of the day (much as sportswear had become streetwear among certain youth subcultures the previous decade), making Lycra a household name and garish hues one of the defining characteristics of the style of the early part of the decade.

Popular culture, including the films *Fame* (1980) (and subsequent TV series of the same name) and *Flashdance* (1983), helped spread the look and even introduce men to the exercise style. With the popularity of the video cassette recorder – not widespread in homes until the Betamax/VHS format wars of the early 1980s – aerobics exercise at home also took off. The likes of the million-selling Jane Fonda's *Workout* (1982) – just one of the film star's 23 exercise videos – or France's ratings hit Sunday morning aerobics show, *Gym Tonic*, with Véronique et Davina, ensured that aerobics style went global. ■

Keeping it box-fresh

IDEA № 47
SNEAKER STYLE

For all that their adoption beyond the sports arena was driven initially by comfort and only then by cool and collectibility, sneakers have rarely been off the radar of either sports technology or pop culture. Yet the street's obsession with sneakers was not planned, any more than it was expected that certain sneakers would be tied to multi-million dollar endorsement deals, supplied in 'limited' editions, or be sold at auction.

Sneakers have also been the stuff of catwalk fashion, with luxury goods companies, including Prada and Louis Vuitton, producing their own versions. But when Bill Bowerman paid 10 dollars to a local graphic artist to design a 'swoosh' logo and co-founded Nike in 1978, his intention was to capitalize on the craze for jogging, ruining countless of his wife's waffle-makers by pouring in clay during his experiments to create a better, bouncier sole.

By the time Peter Moore styled the first Air Jordan in 1984, or sneaker design supremo Tinker Hatfield began devising ways of building air bubbles into soles, sneakers were more than functional. Your 'kicks' of choice, even your brand of choice, said as much about your style allegiance – and, in rougher parts of the United States, your gang allegiance – as did your clothes or hair. 'My sneakers were the hottest things in my wardrobe,' basketball player Walt Frazier once recalled. 'I dug looking down and catching myself walking in them.' And when Run-D.M.C. rapped 'My Adidas' (1986) – and subsequently became the first hip hop stars,

fat laces and all, to collaborate with a sportswear company – they expressed the kind of passion that prefigured that of the so-called 'sneakerheads', who collected and kept countless unworn 'box-fresh' pairs. There would even be demand for fictional sneakers: in 2011 Nike created the Nike Mag, a limited-edition replica of the futuristic sneakers worn by Marty McFly in *Back to the Future II* (1989) when the character time-travelled to 2015.

Street fashion would embrace the sneaker with a see-saw shift between stripped-down 'old school' styles – such as the Converse Chuck Taylor All Star, launched in 1917, or the Vans chequerboard skate shoe (1966) – and highly technological models, in looks as much as construction, from Nike's toe-separating Air Rift to Reebok's pneumatic Pump through to Puma's Disc, with its lace-free tightening mechanism. 'The cachet of sports shoes is that they're fashion but actually do something too,' Tinker Hatfield noted. 'But I could never have predicted how sneakers could influence popular culture or be a means of self-expression.' ∎

Run-D.M.C., the rap band responsible for kick-starting a revival in old-school Adidas sneakers ('My Adidas' celebrated their love of the brand's shoes), posing for the cover of NME in Philadelphia during the 1980s.

Defining streetwear

IDEA № 48
HIP HOP

If hip hop – as (rivalling country and western) the world's most popular music genre – defined a generation, then the dress of its stars also did more than any other single influence to define the teen uniform. Urban fashion, as it become known within the fashion industry, followed the late 1970s/early 1980s style of African-American youth in hip hop's heartlands – New York, Los Angeles, Chicago, Detroit, Philadelphia, Atlanta – in its influences and preferences.

Initially these included loose-fit clothing, the appropriation of sportswear and work-wear as streetwear, a love of bold colour and branding, and sometimes cartoon excesses – especially in accessories, with everything from jewellery to spectacles writ large. Trends were sometimes left-field, with, for example, rap duo Kris Kross wearing their clothes backwards. Hip hop or urban style was comfortable, but above all it was young and brash; it cried out to be noticed. Even though the clothing was inexpensive, the particularity of one's choices – for example in owning the latest label or a limited edition – ranked one among peers. Even a tracksuit could be a source of one-upmanship.

Indeed, much like many street styles, the clothing choice was often about seeking to ape one's supposed betters – which perhaps explains black, urban hip hop roots' readiness to wear the brands of white, middle-class, preppy America, the likes of Ralph Lauren, Tommy Hilfiger or Nautica. The renegade image was one of success. In turn, white middle-class and suburban kids turned cultural tourists and aped the style of a highly romanticized ghetto life – creating a feedback loop that would help make hip hop style a worldwide phenomenon and, unlike most street fashions of previous generations, one that would cut across ethnic divides too.

Hip hop was also a driving force behind the spread of various street style trends that would take on a life of their own – both those that were niche within the hip hop world, such as gangsta, through to those that would transcend it, from **bling** to tattoos. Such was the potency of hip hop as a musical force and, via the likes of MTV and YouTube, a visual force as well – that, almost inevitably, by the 2000s many leading hip hop stars had launched their own clothing lines, from Russell Simmons's groundbreaking Phat Farm, through to Jay-Z and Damon Dash's Rocawear and Sean Combs's Sean John, among many others. The moves only cemented the idea of hip hop as the dominant influence in shaping global teen style. ■

TOP: *Hip hop beanie, hip hop goatee and hip hop outsized, XXL jacket, complete with hip hop gang-style finger action.*

ABOVE: *The Untouchable Force Organization's The Kangol Kid (wearing, appropriately, early hip hop brand favourite Kangol), Mixmaster Ice (in British sports brand Reebok) and Dr. Ice, in New York in 1986. The group were breakers turned rappers, their biggest hit being hip hop classic 'Roxanne, Roxanne'.*

OPPOSITE: *LL Cool J – also a fan of Kangol, specifically its bucket hat – in Adidas sneakers and plenty of bling, performing in Philadelphia during the 1980s.*

A bass player performing in London's Covent Garden mixes exaggerated takes on 50s Rockabilly – the hair, the tattoos, the neckerchief – with heavy metal and punk influences such as the studded belt and leather trousers.

1950s with a dark twist

IDEA Nº 49
PSYCHOBILLY

Take rockabilly – an exaggerated style inspired by 1950s Americana – and cross it with 1960s garage, 1970s punk, extreme hairstyles, excess tattoos and a love of the lurid, and the unlikely result is psychobilly. Few street style subcultures can claim to be as unexpected a hybrid – especially when, as is the case with some elements of psychobilly, also informed by an interest in horror themes, zombies and skull motifs (which, of course, nods to the B-movie culture of the 1950s too). But psychobilly also brought together elements of Teddy boy (crepe-soled shoes), skinhead (flight jackets and Dr. Martens boots), and punk (customized leather and tartan).

The term is said to have been first used by American band the Cramps – the coinage actually belonging to a Johnny Cash song lyric – but it was popularized during the early 1980s by pioneering self-described psychobilly band the Meteors, from south London. Their fans, as befits the 'psycho' tag, called themselves 'crazies'. Indeed, despite the links to rockabilly (psychobilly bands often conform to the traditional three-piece line-up, with drums, guitar and stand-up double bass), perhaps it was the comic-book oddness of the look of bands like the Polecats, King Kurt and Demented Are Go that meant the genre did not cross over from Britain into the United States and mainland Europe and Japan until the 1990s.

The hyped rockabilly look takes on Betty Page pin-up dressing, a touch of rocker studded black leather and leopard-print Lurex, leggings and miniskirts for women, and extra-large rocker quiffs dyed synthetic shades, big belt buckles, ripped jeans, battered sneakers and zombie graphic T-shirts for men – and with tattoos, horror-inspired or in reverence of particular psychobilly bands, for both. It is a look that would have seemed like a plain twisted take on a

recognizably home-grown style to many Americans or, at best, a perverse mash-up. If a rockabilly girl wears a dress with a polka dot print, a psychobilly one wears skull motifs on hers, in a look where glamour meets *The Munsters*. ∎

ABOVE: *Psychobilly men, characterized most clearly by the height and precision of their 50s-inspired hairstyles, at a Viva Las Vegas weekend in 2006. And psychobilly women in Santiago, Chile, in 2008, all black leather, denim, red lipstick and two-tone hair.*

Covered up and undercover

RIGHT: *A youth wearing a hoodie – accessorized by that other totem of delinquency, the potentially dangerous Staffordshire bull terrier – at home in London in 2006.*

IDEA № 50
THE HOODIE

The cover of the rap group Wu-Tang Clan's 1993 album *Enter the Wu-Tang* perhaps suggests why the hoodie came to evoke the sinister: it shows a horror-style image of a group of faceless, hooded figures. Of course, since it shrouds the face in darkness, the hood has long had such a connotation. The hoodie is, perhaps, a mask for modern times.

This was not so much the case when the hoodie was first worn, when it was more appreciated for affording cheap comfort and protection without being bulky – precisely the qualities offered when the American manufacturer Champion first added the hood to one of its heavyweight sweatshirts in the 1950s. Indeed, it was worn by anyone working in inclement weather, labourers as much as athletes. Its use in high-school athletics in the United States gave the hoodie a kind of innocence.

That changed, however, when sportswear's general adoption by fashion saw the hoodie cross over from track to street in the mid- to late 1970s. Then the anonymity it afforded was quickly appreciated by those wanting to keep a low profile, be they **graffiti** artists, skaters trespassing to ride private spaces or – more sinisterly – those who were in the United States termed 'stick-up kids' (which is to say those who mugged at gunpoint). All three groups rejected mainstream culture and the hoodie became symbolic of some degree of criminality or intimidation – a rejection further underpinned by the hoodie's adoption by hardcore rap in the 1990s.

The hoodie would go on to live parallel lives – on the one side, designer versions giving a certain high-fashion credibility, and the wearing of the hoodie by countless millions of ordinary pre-teen and teenage college kids – notably in the US, where the hoodie might come emblazoned with the college football team name; on the other side, the hood continuing to carry negative symbolism, and internationally too.

In the banlieues of Paris and the tougher inner-city estates of London, media attention saw the hoodie come to represent disaffected youth. In 2006, future British prime minister David Cameron's attempt at improved social integration was dubbed 'hug a hoodie'. And some suggested that when an unarmed 17-year-old, Trayvon Martin, was shot and killed by a neighbourhood watch volunteer in Florida in 2012, the shooter's action was prompted not by anything Martin was doing, but as a result of the assumptions the shooter made about Martin's intentions as a consequence of his dress. Martin was wearing a hoodie. ∎

'In the banlieues of Paris and the tougher inner-city estates of London, media attention saw the hoodie come to represent disaffected youth.'

Ease of movement

RIGHT: *The sportswear is worn for comfort and mobility, both essential to successful breaking. The headbands are part of this 1986 look – one shared with the aerobics boom of the period. The hug-myself pose, however, is pure hip hop.*

OPPOSITE: *These British teenagers show off icons of mid-1980s hip hop: the tracksuits – by Adidas, as Run-D.M.C. would have insisted – following functional sportswear crossover into fashion, and the graffiti-customized 'ghetto blaster'.*

IDEA № 51

BREAKING

Part gymnastics, part martial art – both cited as inspirations by its pioneers, such as the Rock Steady Crew – breaking developed during the 1970s as the improvisational acrobatic dance style to accompany hip hop beats.

Martial arts are a particularly apposite reference, given that breaking was often performed as a so-called 'battle', with dancers taking it in turns to out-dance each other during the 'breaks', the long instrumental/beats-only sections mixed into a DJ set, which became as much a display of the DJ's skills as the dancers'. By 1990, breaking had long transcended the streets of New York's Manhattan and South Bronx on which it was born and had become an international style. Germany hosted the first Battle of the Year in 1990.

Like other aspects of hip hop, the clothing of breaking has since been subsumed by a wider streetwear aesthetic, with breakers favouring the ubiquitous hoodie, outsized T-shirt, loose khakis or cargo pants and sneakers. But its earlier incarnation, while still embedded in sportswear, took on a more particular bent. This was in part practical – smooth nylon tracksuits, and sometimes fitted cycling tops, were worn as much for their lack of resistance against the temporary cardboard or linoleum surface on which the dancing might be done, as they were for ease of movement, while light Adidas sneakers, with fat laces, were equally essential for such athleticism.

But, while other b-boy ('break boy') choices also had a functionality, they often added up to an outlandish-seeming ensemble. Headgear such as a beanie, trucker cap, bandana or even Kangol beret made head-spins possible, while fingerless gloves – borrowed from cycling or weightlifting – protected the palms. But both made for an unlikely mix with a tracksuit. White gloves might be worn – by poppers, in particular, practitioners of a jerky dance style offshoot – to accentuate the movement, much as mime artists might use them. Ski goggles just made a statement. Certainly the style was a long way from the glitzy showbiz version imagined by the 1984 movie *Breakdance*; even the media-created term 'breakdance' is shunned by most breakers. ∎

LEFT: *Breakers in action in New York in 1981. The Kangol hat provides protection for head-spins in breaking's natural environment – the street.*

Mexican expression

IDEA № 52
CHOLOS

The name may have political connotations, deriving as it does from a pejorative term for someone of racially mixed origin, with its deeper roots in a word meaning 'slave', but cholo style is one of the most distinctive in the United States, and one widely hijacked by popular culture.

Growing out of the Mexican-American empowerment movement of the 1960s and 1970s, from the 1990s cholo would become a striking inner-city look adopted specifically by gang members of Mexican descent (though the term was also applied to Hispanics and Filipinos) in the American Southwest – from California to Colorado and south to New Mexico.

The predominantly male style might be described as a cross between the early skater stereotype and hip hop attire but both bigger and more prescriptive: work boots or sneakers, often more old-school than high-tech; bandana, folded flat across the fore-head, or beanie, pulled low over cropped or slicked-back hair; wallet chain; khakis or work pants by the likes of Ben Davis Gorilla Cut or Dickies, worn several sizes too big, held aloft but slung low by a webbing belt; white 'wife-beater' vests worn under outsize short-sleeved work or plaid flannel shirts, typically done up only at the neck. Attention to detail and pride in one's appearance was important: both trousers and shirts would be pressed for sharp creases, and starch often used to provide additional lasting crispness.

More distinctively still, at least on a grown man, was the cholo combination of baggy khaki shorts with bright white socks

pulled up to the knee, especially when accessorized with a low-rider – a low-seated, high-handlebarred and fully customized bicycle. The look was invariably finished off with an armful – or neckful – of black ink, fine-line tattoos, a style of tattooing that alone set off a spate of celebrity emulation in the early 2000s.

Even among self-proclaimed cholos, dress was more likely a lifestyle choice than a means of identifying oneself as a gang member, and when given a female twist, was

as likely to be seen on the likes of Gwen Stefani, Pink and the Black Eyed Peas' Fergie as hanging on a Los Angeles street corner demanding respect. It was also given a more fashion-conscious spin in Tokyo, where cholo, complete with brandishing of the Mexican flag, became a subculture during the first decade of the twenty-first century ∎

ABOVE: *The Mexican Day Parade down Madison Avenue in New York gives full vent to cholo style, most notably in the riding of full-chrome, high handle-bar low-riders.*

LEFT: *Three members of the Dog Patch Gang looking intimidating for the camera – note the signature vests, khakis, tattoos and facial hair.*

The anti-Rasta

RIGHT AND BELOW: *Dancehall girls dress to excess with plenty of bling and flesh at ragamuffin events in London's West End in 2004 and, below, in Kingston, Jamaica, in 1997.*

IDEA № 53

RAGGAMUFFINS

If Rasta dress was expressive of religious affiliation – and, more than that, of a spiritual outlook on life founded on mutual and self-respect – then raggamuffin was its polar opposite. An expression of sex, money, status and violence, it grew up in the early 1980s in Kingston, Jamaica, before making its way across the water to New York and then on to London and the European continent.

As much as **Rasta** style was ring-fenced by its spiritual leanings, so raggamuffin, or just 'ragga', style was brash (the word is an intentional misspelling and ironic mutation of 'ragamuffin', a pejorative nineteenth-century colonial term meaning someone tattered and scruffy). For men, that might mean loud, colourful clothing, ostentatious (if, on closer inspection, often faux) jewellery

and so-called 'click suits' – made from patchworks of heavily embroidered, stonewashed, **distressed** denim. For women the emphasis was on the glitzy, sexualized and, above all, revealing: bejewelled bra tops, thigh-high boots, fishnet and other semitransparent layers, 'batty-rider' shorts (which is to say, very short ones) and a preference for ostensibly rich, textural materials, from velvet and

lace to leather and suede, as well as skin-tight Lycra and denim, often combined in unexpected, eclectic, inventive ways.

Indeed, the gaudy style of raggamuffin was best suited for the clubs its devotees attended – dressing for show in the place to show off, to dance, in suitably provocative fashion, to the ragga music that celebrated sex and excess. But the look's readiness to mix up different, often clashing items would find wider influence, notably among West Indian teens in the UK during the 1990s. There, cheek by jowl, it would even influence the Indian and Pakistani communities to create what was termed bhangramuffin, a heightened version of the more spectacular elements of traditional Punjabi (Indian/Pakistani) dress worn in a new way by British Asian youth. ■

Raggamuffin's embracing of excess – as typified by this woman's jewellery and her rhinestone-patterned bra top – was, among black cultures, the antithesis of Rasta.

'The gaudy style of raggamuffin was best suited for the clubs its devotees attended – dressing for show in the place to show off.'

Theatrical extravagance

IDEA №54
NEW ROMANTICISM

As a statement, New Romanticism was a sign of the times, specifically 1980s Britain: an extravagant, theatrical form of dress that was both a stark contrast to the more dour styles of the previous decade (such as Two Tone and skinhead) or the nihilism of punk, and a style that seemed to bridge societal shifts, both as escapism from recession and then as an expression of a consumer boom.

The name – coined in 1981 by Richard James Burgess, the original producer of band Spandau Ballet – said it all, suggesting both a break from the past and a style that suggested anything goes, as long as the idea of escapism and performance trumped concerns for practicality or politics. Florid, futuristic, piratical, pantomimic, New Romanticism was dressing to decadent, almost cartoon, excess. With its gender-bending, make-up and colour, it was the 1980s answer to glam: shoulders were wide, boots high, shirts ruffled, hats worn, with

any of history's style archetypes – from cowboy to pirate to Rob Roy rebel – a possible source of inspiration.

Although New Romanticism was not alone in pursuing this sense of performance – goth and 'alternative' style also came through at the same time – the term came to encapsulate a defining look of the first half of the decade, its dominant club culture and the wave of post-punk acts like Adam and the Ants (styled by Vivienne Westwood and briefly managed by punk impresario Malcolm McLaren) and synth-pop acts such as Duran Duran, Culture Club, Visage and Spandau Ballet.

It was in clubland and through the music industry that New Romanticism took off, in particular through Billy's (later Gossips) in London's Soho, at which Steve Strange launched a midweek club night in 1978. This later moved to a Covent Garden wine bar called the Blitz, complete with World War II-inspired decor. Far from needing the money to get in, Strange door policy – at one point enforced by Culture Club's Boy George – was that anyone hoping to become a 'Blitz Kid' had to be impressively dressed.

Since these club nights espoused the notion of status through self-expressive style – rather than through spending power, as was the mantra of the so-called 'designer decade' – the idea of holding them on Tuesday nights gave them a certain exclusivity. ∎

ABOVE: *A New Romantic – the flamboyant, theatrical dress, the outlandish make-up and dramatic hair – at the pioneering Blitz Club in London in 1981.*

BELOW: *Designer Stephen Linard and milliner Stephen Jones at the St. Moritz Club, London, in 1980.*

ABOVE: *Perhaps the definitive New Romantic band, Spandau Ballet.*

The global teen uniform

IDEA № 55
SKATEBOARDING

For some it was little more than a fad; for others the origins of a public nuisance and a health risk. But what the skateboard started was far-reaching – a lifestyle that has spawned skateboard art, skate bands (playing thrash rock), video games and, most pervasively, from the late 1970s on, a clear skater style.

In 1963 a competition, the first of its kind, was held on Hermosa Beach, California. It involved young men staying upright on an 18-centimetre (7-inch) -wide board mounted on four small wheels. In 1959, the Roller Derby skateboard, the first mass-market skateboard, had gone on sale. Skateboarding became a pop cultural phenomenon: three million boards would be sold in the run up to the Hermosa event. Although the voice of safety experts by 1965 brought the first wave of skateboarding to an end, it increased in popularity again from the mid-1970s onwards, with new designs, new materials and an evolving style.

Skateboarding was often known as 'side-walk surfing' in its early days: the sport had its origins in West Coast surfing and borrowed its look – it was certainly comfort-oriented and loose-fitting, but also bold, perennially youthful and, then at least, symbolic of skateboarding's rebel spirit. The skill itself involves thrills and spills; the sport was ahead of the pack in its crossover interest in tattooing, **indie** music and other subcultures. In its earlier days outcast skaters defied the law to develop their talents; although soon commercialized, skate culture retained a strong underground element, with fanzines staying true to the original DIY approach, when the first boards were made by cannibalizing roller skates and bits of plywood. This approach also kick-started skatewear as a major fashion category, with garage screen-printing and back-room customization of menswear basics.

Skateboarding made accessible for mainstream fashion the combat trouser, hoodie and wallet chain, the beanie hat and trucker cap, the outsize T-shirt, super-baggy jeans and its own dedicated genre of sneaker, each a street trend in its own right and each in time made global – in part by media interest in the sport following its being put on a high-level competitive footing, in part by the adoption of the look by hip hop. Skateboarding's own sub-styles were equally influential – the thrift-store punk skater, for example, in battered retro sneakers, checked shirt, rock-band T-shirt, workwear trousers, windbreaker and mesh baseball cap, all making the style effectively a predecessor to grunge. They are also indicative of how skaters moved their style on once it had entered the mass market. ∎

ABOVE: *Where else to practise but in the empty swimming pools of abandoned properties (or those whose owners were simply out)? Pool riders in action in Rialto, California, in 1998.*

LEFT: *Skatboarder Rafael Leffa, boarding near Bank, London in 2008, wearing archetypal skateboard clothing, loose t-shirt, baggy jeans and sneakers.*

'In its earlier days outcast skaters defied the law to develop their talents.'

Ripped jeans offer the possibility of sexual suggestibility, artfully placed rips allowing glimpses of the flesh beneath, as these jeans – more rip than denim – suggest in a shot reminiscent of the cover of The Rolling Stones' Sticky Fingers album cover.

Old before its time

IDEA Nº 56
DISTRESSING

When commercially distressed clothes – which is to say those that have been deliberately frayed, faded, ripped and aged – first appeared in the early 1980s, the idea was considered faintly ridiculous. To wear something that looked old and worn went against fashion's then love of the bold and brash, its 1980s philosophy of power dressing and wealth display.

To pay – and heavily, given how labour-intensive this faux ageing was to achieve convincingly – for an item that already looked old without the benefit of years of good service seemed counter to luxury's standard notions of perfection. As Renzo Rosso, founder of Italian casualwear company Diesel and pioneer of distressing techniques, would put it: '[Business] was so hard at first. People would send the clothes back, thinking they were faulty. Now everyone gets why a pair of jeans already comes looking worn out. Back then it was crazy.'

More avant-garde designers – including Comme des Garçons, Dries van Noten, Martin Margiela and Hussein Chalayan – would subsequently embrace various methods of partial destruction of their clothes (from burying them to shooting at them to launching fireworks off them), though more for artistic effect than to create an illusion of ageing. Although also long affected by the upper classes – among whom a slightly abraded or 'foxed' shirt collar saved one from the faux pas of having clothes that looked too new – it was in street and casual fashion that distressing would reach an apex of both technique (the use of power tools, specially developed acids and washes, wire-brushing, baking, laser abrasion) and sophistication. Denim led the way: stone-washing was one of the earliest techniques (literally washing the denim with pumice stone in specially reinforced drums), developed to give a worn-out look specifically to a raw fabric that was so hard to wear out. But it

was applied to other garments and fabrics too to introduce rips, fraying, fading and staining, creating a look whose various permutations moved in and out of fashion over the following decades – often, it is said, in line with the health of the economy (distressing mirroring more boom times).

The demand for clothes that looked old before their time was in part about credibility, conferring a coolness factor in seemingly having lived in a garment to the point where each hole and mark could tell a story; such clothing cut against fashion's gloss and impersonality, in a similar way to punk's DIY aesthetic. Distressing's texture and decoration without pattern also appealed. But it was just as much a symptom of **fast fashion**. With wardrobes ever expanding as globalization made clothing ever cheaper, and trends turning over at breakneck pace, the opportunity to actually wear a garment sufficiently often for it to show real signs of ageing became rarer. With the uptake of **vintage** as a fashion category in its own right in the early 2000s, faking the old became ever more desirable for those who could not find the genuinely old and more artful forms of distressing – to subtly age a garment, for example, rather than for outright effect – came into use. ■

ABOVE: *Jonathan Knight of American boy band New Kids on the Block, sporting jeans ripped well beyond the possibility of wear and tear, in New York in 1985.*

Conspicuous consumption

IDEA № 57
BLING

Originating in the hip hop community, bling refers to ostentatious and flashy jewellery and personal ornamentation – gold ropes and diamonds, bejewelled watches and cell phones, even gold or diamond-studded teeth. This unashamed expression of personal wealth through jewellery was perhaps especially important to the rappers that popularized the word, as the rise from the relative poverty of the streets to considerable wealth and, most importantly, hyper-conspicuous consumption is central to rap mythology.

Indeed, showing the world that you have escaped your beginnings in a way that might well be considered excessive, cartoony or vulgar underpins what bling is all about. It is arguably all the more significant in a world in which expressing this through obviously expensive clothing is not an option: jewellery is a way of distinguishing yourself from the teenager equally free to wear the same mass-market sneakers and sportswear. Certain jewellers, such as David Shiminov of Kinetics New York and Jacob Arabo, built major businesses catering to this market.

Culturally, such has been bling's importance that, as rapper 50 Cent put it in 'I Got Money' (2007), it is like 'blaow', a street slang term meaning giving a feeling similar to a drug-induced high. Stylistically bling became such a pillar of rap dress that, ironically, wearing imitation gold and gems became the only option for the less well-off who wanted to keep pace with the look. Yet 'bling' – a term that dates in rap to 1988, and went mainstream in the mid- to late 1990s – suggests the brightness of real gold and cut diamonds, not plastic.

Through the 2000s the term 'bling' became widely used as hip hop rose to become the world's best-selling genre of music. It was even used in verb form, with 'to bling up' suggesting the **customization** of products to make them more flashy, or more gaudy, depending on taste: cheap crystals, for example, could be added to accessories to achieve the desired sparkling effect. By then, however, the rap world itself had largely ceased to use the word or pursue the look; in 2005 Public Enemy even narrated a short film explaining the deadly repercussions of the trade in blood diamonds that bling in part underpinned. ∎

British rapper Slick Rick, seen here with his precious metal piled on in trademark style.

Criminality as cool

IDEA № 58

GANG CULTURE

'Gee, Officer Krupke', Stephen Sondheim's song from 1957's *West Side Story* – a tale of love hindered by street gang rivalry – may put a comic spin on the issue, but by the 1950s so-called juvenile delinquency, or the 'social disease' as Sondheim put it, had become a genuine public concern. *West Side Story*'s characterizing of the Jets and the Sharks through their dress, however, was not the first time a connection between criminality or delinquency and cool had been made.

ABOVE: *Gang culture has long underpinned a certain bad boy style, as with this example, in cap and t-shirt - akin to the look of Brando in* The Wild One, *yet dating from 1925 in Paris.*

BELOW: *Gang members from the Bloods attend the 'Cures Not Wars' marijuana march in New York in 2001, an event aiming to legalize marijuana. The gang members wear their red bandanas, symbolic of their gang membership, to hide their faces.*

The Teddy boys, rockers, mods, **skinheads** and casuals were all, in turn, style tribes associated with criminal behaviour, their very clothing coming to signify as much to some. Yet before them all, the so-called Apache gangs of Paris, during the closing decades of the nineteenth century, were pictured by the popular press of the time as identifiable by their style: dramatically tapered 'Lafont' cord trousers, cropped, thick work jackets (often furled around an arm to act as a shield during knife fights), Breton-type tops or flannel shirts, leather bracelets and a garment that identified their allegiance, typically a certain colour of scarf.

That idea was resonant in the street gangs of Los Angeles almost a century later, not only in the wearing of specific colours of bandana or 'rag' – the Crips associated with blue and/or black, for example, the Bloods with red – but also in how it was worn, or in which back pocket it was carried. Tattoos were used to denote gang affiliation, and so too certain plaids, belt buckles, team jackets, certain colours of laces and even, for women, of nail polish. The same gangs would also use old sneakers as a means of marking gang territory, throwing them over telephone wires, where they would hang by the laces indefinitely.

By the 1990s, gang style, or an imagined echoing of it, would become a trope of street style of such depth that its origins would be lost to many who followed it: for example, the wearing of sneakers without laces, and the wearing of sweat pants or trousers low-slung and typically without a belt, stemmed from laces and belts being confiscated by the police from those arrested to prevent their use either as weapons or as means of suicide. Even badges of genuine criminality, rather than a romantic if ill-considered mimicking of them, could prove desirable symbols of outsider status – electronic ankle tags, deployed with the introduction of the ASBO (Anti-Social Behaviour Order) by the British government in 1998, might well be worn with a certain twisted pride. ■

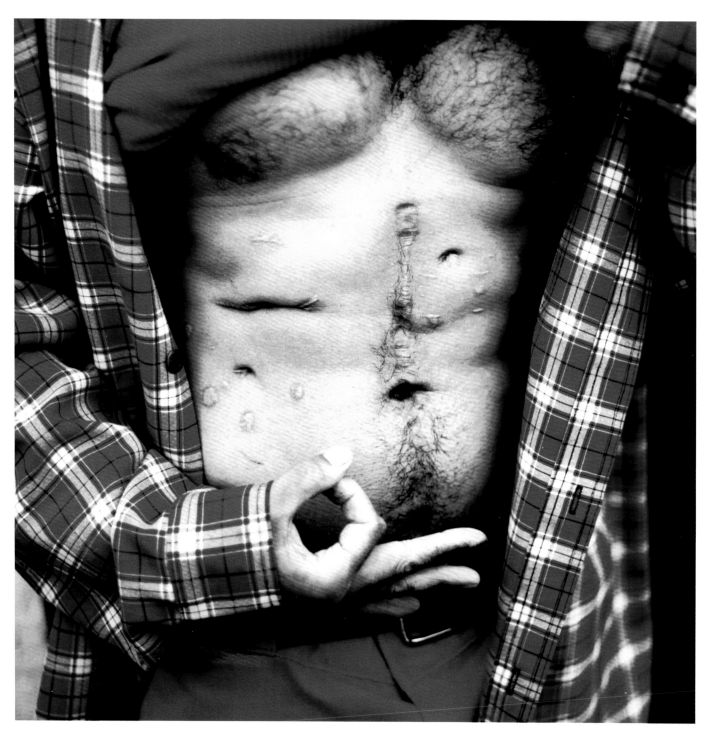

Gang style typically sees the over-shirt worn undone, but here that is to startling effect: a Blood gang member (giving the gang sign) reveals the scars of having been shot and stabbed 23 times, and living to show it off.

The dark side

IDEA № 59

GOTH

Cross a love of horror movies and bondage and any resulting subculture might not be expected to last too long. Goth, however, topped all expectations and has become one of the most enduring and widely followed youth movements since it originated in the 1980s, taking its name, and its cues – somewhat against the decade's rise of polished, mostly upbeat designer wear – from the gothic horror romance of the Victorian period, from Mary Shelley's *Frankenstein* to Edgar Allan Poe's *The Raven*.

BELOW: *The Victorian period gave rise to gothic horror as a genre of fiction – from* Frankenstein *to* Dracula *– which, in turn, has shaped the 'period dress' of more sartorial goths.*

Goth's darkness, sombre overtones and almost comically humourless image played to stereotypes of teen angst, disillusion and the desire to be different (though not too different). But goth, developing out of the post-punk period, proved to be more sophisticated, intellectual and nuanced than its Victorian theatricality, its flamboyant yet sombre dressing – corsets and lace mittens, capes and ruffled cuffs, top hats, frock coats and crucifixes, black-dyed hair, pale skin, dark eye make-up and black nail varnish (for men and women alike) – or its leanings towards the supernatural (vampirism especially) perhaps suggested.

Embraced simultaneously in the United States – in the coastal big cities at least – and across the UK, bands such as Joy Division and, more obviously, Bauhaus, the Sisters of Mercy, Fields of Nephilim, the Cure, Siouxsie and the Banshees and the Mission won the backing of progressive, influential record labels, including Factory Records and Beggars Banquet Records, and embraced experimental production and instrumentation. Goth's field of reference was also highly literary, often citing the likes of pioneering horror writers Edgar Allen Poe and H.P. Lovecraft and the dark, shadowy German expressionist cinema of the 1920s and early 1930s – *Nosferatu*, *The Cabinet of Dr Caligari*, *Metropolis* and *M* among its seminal films.

Small wonder that goth – highbrow, extravagant and seemingly obsessed with the themes of darkness and death – should find appeal among young people trying to find themselves. Nor perhaps is it surprising that it, like many youth subcultures, should have been widely misunderstood, in goth's case too readily associated with violence and self-harm, sometimes even attracting prejudice as a result. ■

The search for authenticity

IDEA № 60
ACID JAZZ

Anecdote has it that DJ Gilles Peterson put on an old rare groove record at a 1987 'Talkin' Loud Sayin' Something' club session and gradually speeded it up until the sound became distorted. His fellow DJ Chris Bangs picked up a microphone and suggested, tongue in cheek, that if other music of the era was 'acid house', then this must be 'acid jazz'.

A new genre was born: a break with the 'soulless' electronic music favoured at the time and a return to real instrumentation by blending other genres of the past, from funk to bebop and free jazz, mambo to dub. And, in keeping, so was a new, equally eclectic clothing style. The look was part contemporary, with leanings towards 'old school' skater/rapper sportswear, including traditional tracksuits and reissued trainers, and part retro, with more sartorial leanings towards a Blue Note jazz-cool style of 1940s/1950s-era suits, loud ties, polo necks and berets. Additionally, it incorporated

elements of blaxploitation funk, all colourful wide-collared shirts and hip-hugging flares, and of mod, with neat suede-fronted cardigans, pork-pie hats, bowling shoes and slim, ankle-skimming trousers (the latter element driven by Eddie Piller, co-founder of the influential Acid Jazz independent record label that would shape the scene).

While acid jazz style might take credit for one of fashion's first serious reappraisals of vintage clothing, and while it may have been as much of a new hybrid as the music, what pulled together the diverse components was, as with **northern soul** before it,

a high regard for authenticity – even if the attention to period detail might cross several periods on the same dance floor. The music – both remixed originals and new music from the likes of the James Taylor Quartet, Brand New Heavies, Galliano, Corduroy and Jamiroquai (with lead singer Jay Kay's reputation for distinctive headgear) – and fashion alike took styles from the past and, with some unexpected contrasts and juxtapositions, made them modern in the blending. ∎

ABOVE: *A guest at an acid jazz/rare groove night in the UK during the 1980s (above), his headgear perhaps marking him out as a follower of the style, as it did the singer of Jamiroquai (left), becoming part of his own early signature look.*

Off the grid, out of fashion

IDEA № 61

TRAVELLERS

Wilfully rejecting fashion and having (or feigning) no interest in style can, ironically, lead to a distinctive look. And for the New Age traveller, extreme green eco-campaigner or so-called crusty, this was defined by their unkempt appearance – a product perhaps of living on the road, on narrowboats, in mobile homes, converted trucks and buses, campsites, short-term squats or other forms of cheap, 'off the grid' accommodation.

It was also seen in their embracing the alternative in personal appearance long before it entered the mainstream, from tattoos to piercings, long and/or brightly coloured hair and dreadlocks, to second-hand, cheap and hard-wearing army surplus boots and clothing (often dyed black to remove militaristic implications), face paint, patchwork and other garments of uncertain ethnic inspiration.

Versions of the traveller and travelling communities have existed for centuries, especially across Europe – firing the artistic imagination especially in the early twentieth century, when models might be dressed in Romani Gypsy style for the fashionable portraiture of the period. From the late 1970s onwards, however, the traveller represented a post-hippie and post-punk hybrid distinctive to the UK, in part because the free festival scene provided a focus for gatherings and alternative thinking. This was as much in their approach to clothing – a rejection of societal norms – as in their New Age spiritual ideology. Their sometimes anarchic dress reflected a rejection of Western society's emphasis on materialism, its unchecked use of natural resources and the damage it causes to both the environment and landscape (with which the traveller lifestyle claimed a certain affinity). It was also a rejection of the traditional family unit and conventional ideas of making progress in life.

Their rejection of such ideas largely saw travellers rejected, in turn, by society, demeaned as 'tree huggers' or 'eco-warriors'; more than simply scrufy, their way of dress came to be characterized as unhygienic. In the UK by the mid-1980s that polarity of lifestyles led to direct opposition from the government of the day and confrontation with the police.

Travellers, however, arguably had the last laugh when much of their key, ahead-of-its-time thinking – in particular on the environment and sustainability – was picked up during the 1990s by the wider public. It was also reflected by some of the more progressive elements of the fashion industry, in, for example, the increasing use of organic cotton and focus on ethical manufacturing. ∎

The style of the Parisian bourgeoisie

IDEA Nº 62
BCBG

First there were *The Official Preppy Handbook* (1980) and *The Sloane Ranger Handbook* (1982), both of which codified the dress – in a tongue-in-cheek manner – of the well-to-do upper and upper-middle classes of, respectively, America's East Coast WASP communities and Britain's west London and Home Counties. And then in 1986 came the French version: Thierry Mantoux's *BCBG: Le guide du bon chic bon genre* – 'good style, good class'.

This was the Parisian style of the wealthy Right Bank (rather than the intellectual, countercultural Left Bank) that espoused polish, good breeding, good grooming and a uniform of classic luxe items beloved across generations – the cashmere sweater and mackintosh, ballet pumps and Hermès Birkin bag, silk scarves, kilts and twin-set knits, school satchels, pearl necklaces and expensive watches. This French preppy – though more sophisticated and with the emphasis more on the woman than the man – continued to define the sartorial look of the French capital through the 1990s: beyond fashion because it was above fashion. Like preppy, however, the way the key items were worn was as much a signifier of the wearer's being – or aspiring to be – part of an elite as what was worn: as preppy polo shirts were worn collar turned up, so too was one's mannish shirt-blouse collar.

BCBG was found in any of the Parisian suburbs where the money was: Auteuil, Neuilly, Passy. Indeed, BCBG also came to be known as 'Seizième', after the 16th arrondissement, and 'Versaillais'. And it was in these areas that the symbolism of the style had its greatest power. Here, among its followers, it passed for stylish; to those outside the circle, looking in, it often looked more old-fashioned, the young dressing much like the old, with safe conservatism, which made it all the easier a target for Mantoux's gentle parody. ■

OPPOSITE: *Although the style of BCBG took hold in the 1980s, in the new century it was still going strong, as seen in this street fashion shot during Paris Fashion Week in 2013.*

ABOVE: *If stereotype has students as favouring basic, scruffy and second-hand clothing, BCBG students still manage to look like fashion plates, as here with these two in Paris in 1986.*

LEFT: *BCBG was fundamentally a class-oriented style: upper middle-class, as opposed to street-style's usual working class origins. Here in 1978, before BCBG became codified, it is worn by Parisian public relations executive Countess Angelika Lazensky.*

Awaydays for exotic labels

RIGHT: *Casual in part introduced the idea of the brand and its logo being as important to clothing's appeal as the garment itself – here a casual proudly shows off the label on his Lyle & Scott sweater.*

BELOW: *Casuals group at a subway entrance in Wanstead, east London, in 1983. Blousons, faded jeans, polo shirts worn done up at the neck, branded knitwear – all were part of the casual wardrobe.*

IDEA Nº 63

CASUALS

Its origins have been hotly debated – some say London, some say the big cities of England's Northwest – but casual, as the mid-1970s to early 1980s British movement was generally termed (among regional variations including 'Perry boys', 'scallies' and 'dressers') was groundbreaking in its introduction of sportswear to everyday fashion, certainly pre-empting hip hop's doing so in the United States.

In the search for working-class sartorial one-upmanship, exotic new foreign sportswear labels were favoured – the very labels that had become newly accessible to young football fans now travelling abroad to watch their teams' away matches. Much like the mods before, with their emphasis on the new and on constant change, so casuals would turn the football terraces into a weekly catwalk of their latest selections. But while mod and other British style subcultures remain better known, arguably casual was considerably more important in terms of shaping the standard small-c casual style of British men for the decades that followed.

Every sport was examined for the possibilities of its boldest, brashest, most colourful and graphic clothing – none of them characteristics that could be applied to standard menswear at the time. Golf gave casuals Pringle and Lyle & Scott, tennis gave them Slazenger, Ellesse and Fila, sailing Henri Lloyd, and outdoor pursuits such brands as Berghaus and Timberland. The style was also about rediscovering long-established authentic brands that had fallen into general disregard or long been written off as an old man's choice (Farah, Burberry, Aquascutum), and pioneering what would become an international interest in mostly Italian designer labels such as Armani, Cerruti and Valentino. Those awaydays would often present the opportunity to shoplift them, until local authorities wised up to the sudden loss of stock on certain Saturdays.

Casual may have been concerned with wearing the right logos before brand identity had become a major aspect of the fashion industry; brands had a fleeting fashionability within casual circles and had to be right for your region, since different teams' fans wore different labels. But how the clothes were styled was as much part of it: wide-wale cords, for example, might be split at the seam so they sat better over one's rare Adidas trainers, or cut and not hemmed so as to create a fringe of loose threads; shirts would be worn buttoned to the neck. And the labels would be accessorized with more outlandish garments too: a deerstalker hat perhaps, or a fisherman's coat, worn with enough attitude to carry them off. Indeed, the casual look could be as formal as it could be esoteric, incorporating smart blazers and pressed (or even Sta-Prest) trousers. ∎

Casual was unusual among British style cultures in being a scene that came out of football rather than out of music.

BELOW AND OPPOSITE: The style press has become an established sector in magazine publishing internationally, as these covers, from magazines in the UK, France, Japan and the US show. The cover of The Face, opposite, second row, far right, gives an example of Ray Petri's Buffalo style.

IDEA № 64
THE STYLE PRESS

With the launch of the fashion, music and style magazine *The Face* in the UK in 1980, its founder Nick Logan did a great deal more than merely steer youth-oriented publications away from their emphasis on music and towards those topics that also took in the nature of youth style.

'I'm a fan and I know the excitement of being caught up with something new,' Logan said at the launch of his new publication, which was named after the mod term for an individual who sets the pace in fashion terms. 'I need a magazine. I enjoy having my finger right on the pulse. It's so easy to lose touch. What *The Face* does is combine racy copy with a lot of photography – people do underestimate the power of good pictures.'

The former editor of music magazines *NME* and *Smash Hits* gave youth culture a voice only previously found in niche fanzines, a voice that – pre-youth TV, pre-internet, pre-**social media** – would capture a new energy among teens to late 20-somethings. *The Face* would also inspire countless imitators both nationally and internationally, including *i-D* and *Dazed & Confused* in the UK, *Numéro* and *Les Inrockuptibles* in France, and, later, *Fruits* and *Free & Easy* in Japan. It also helped open the way for similar style-centred titles for an older audience, such as *Arena* in the UK.

Certainly the magazine courted youthful, ebullient controversy: in 1992 it was sued by Jason Donovan, an actor and singer, for casting doubt on his sexuality; the 1996 'Usual Suspects' fashion shoot is credited with launching so-called 'heroin chic'; and while the magazine may have been renowned for its progressive art direction – courtesy of graphic designer Neville Brody – it was also criticized for commercializing youth, turning it on to designer clothing and label culture.

But, more importantly, *The Face* created a new genre of magazine that documented street fashion and, in turn, shaped street fashion in a way that no other media had done before. While it was the first to identify style movements such as the New Romantics, it also created them – one example being the creation of 'Buffalo', an influential if short-lived 'non-fashion' style tribe shaped by *Face* stylist Ray Petri and photographer Jamie Morgan through the early 1980s. ∎

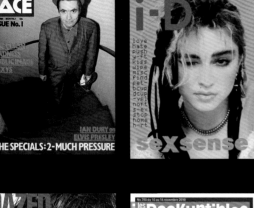

Paying respect to the founding fathers

IDEA № 65
OLD SCHOOL

ABOVE: *British grime MCs Crazy D and P Money gesture to camera at a drum and base rave in London Bridge, London, in 2011. Crazy D's t-shirt is a graphic pun on the Run-D.M.C. logo, said to be designed by Def Jam's founder Rick Rubin and the band, and counted as one of the most widely recognized band logos.*

Rapper 2Pac's intro to his 'Old School' track (1995) neatly summed up the street idea of 'old school' (or 'old skool' as it was sometimes written): it was about paying respect to the founding fathers – their music, attitude, art and style – of the tribe to which one felt one belonged, be that rapper, skateboarder, graffiti artist or some other. It was about looking to the past for inspiration, for ideas ready for update and reinvention or revival.

Although the term was sometimes used pejoratively, in most cases it suggested a certain reverence for the sounds and styles of the early days of hip hop and rap in the early 1980s. Such bands as the Sugarhill Gang, Run-D.M.C., LL Cool J and Grandmaster Flash were revered, while in graffiti it was the work being done from the 1970s to the mid-1990s, characterized by bold, colourful tags and bubble lettering. Urban fashion looked back to the trend for outsized graphic

T-shirts, overly baggy denims, baseball caps worn backwards and gold jewellery – a style that, over time, became the stereotype of the urban look and which was celebrated in songs by hip hop singers Ahmad ('Back in the Day', 1994) and Missy Elliott ('Back in the Day', 2003).

Old school sometimes suggested a certain simplicity or naivety in a genre that appealed because it was not only basic and uncluttered but also pioneering – low-tech canvas sneakers would be 'old-school' next to the latest, high-tech models, for example. It also suggested a certain insider knowledge to later generations, who were too young to remember the origins of a look but were embracing old school style as, to them, a new style. Here, indeed, was a term that would go beyond its original eighteenth century meaning – in reference to people of conservative views – and become the urban fashion arena's affectionate term for the original. ∎

BELOW: *The baseball caps, varsity jackets and even the hand gestures all hark back to hip hop's golden years – but worn again, here in the UK in 2006 – appealing to some for nostalgic reasons and, to those too young the first time around, as an expression of rediscovery.*

A teenager in skater style – a culture akin to graffiti art – tags a bridge with a marker pen in the UK, during the 2000s.

Edginess for sale

RIGHT: Stephen Sprouse's neon graffiti-style art was posthumously honoured by Louis Vuitton, the luggage company that in 2004 released a collection using Sprouse's graphic style on its bags.

BELOW: Graffiti at first suggested criminality, then a certain credibility, as shown by this store on New York's Lower East Side during the 1980s.

IDEA № 66
GRAFFITI

Whoever Kilroy was, he made a point. During World War II the phrase 'Kilroy was here' became a widespread piece of graffiti in many parts of the world, so well known that the phrase entered popular culture. But its deeper sense – the affirmation of an individual's existence, made all the more real by their mark left along their life's path – rings true for youth, especially those suffering the stereotyped existential angst.

Simple tagging – leaving a marker-penned, personalized scribble on walls, bus shelters, public transport seating and so on – may lack the art of its more sophisticated cousin graffiti, but it remains a form of expression, perhaps akin to territorial marking. It is one that dates back to times of ancient civilizations, notably the Roman Empire, for whose people it was also a form of dissent.

It would take until the 1970s for graffiti to adopt the parallel experience of being both reappraised as a serious art form (1979 saw graffiti artist Lee Quiñones given the first gallery opening, in Rome, by art dealer Claudio Bruni) and vilified as illegal vandalism. Both forms of credibility, together with graffiti's colourful, bold style and instant association with street culture, inevitably appealed to fashion.

New York graffiti artists such as Haze, Lady Pink and Phase 2 were among the first to transfer their work – especially widely recognizable, cartoon-like characters – to sneakers, hats and jackets. But it would not be long until, in the early 1980s, graffiti as clothing decoration began to trickle up to high fashion, when the pioneering Vivienne Westwood worked with Keith Haring to transfer his street art on to her clothing. And it was a testament to how mainstream graffiti had become by the turn of the millennium that in 2001 Stephen Sprouse worked with Louis Vuitton on its 'Graffiti' collection to bring a form of bold neon tagging to its luxury bags and luggage.

Indeed, while graffiti's legality would remain a grey area, the new century also saw the role of public art reassessed and graffiti's **commercialization** complete, now just another graphic style heavily associated with street style and latent edginess. Inevitably it was co-opted by brand giants within the fashion industry and outside it, each keen to tap the youth market, including Sony, IBM and McDonald's, as well as **extreme sport** and video game companies. ■

A statement against uncertainty

PANINARO

A sandwich bar might not be the most inspiring place for a youth subculture to begin, but Al Panino, in the Duomo San Babila area of Milan, prompted just this during the early 1980s. The culture was subsequently christened 'paninaro' by the newspaper *La Stampa*, its followers 'paninari' – for them it was about the expression of wealth and status through their own carefully curated selection of clothing.

Ironically however, such clothing was not automatically that of the burgeoning Italian designer fashions that, alongside the automotive industry, were helping Italy turn a corner in its postwar economic recovery. Indeed, the flashiness of the paninari – teens and young twenty-something adults – was in some sense a reaction against the drabness of much Italian urban life through the 1950s, '60s and '70s. It also expressed a deliberate aloofness from the political strife and uncertainty that engulfed the nation over these decades: notably the battle between right wing and communistic political extremes and the threat of terrorism.

The paninari, most of whom were from comfortable, middle-class families, underscored their own vision of shallow, cosmopolitan living – la **dolce vita** for beginners – through their fashion choices, which tended to lean towards the colourful and luxurious, worn in an almost stereotyped Italian way: sweaters draped over the shoulders, trousers or denim cut or rolled short to the ankle, no socks, puffa jackets. But they also reflected a certain (apolitical, consumerist) nationalism; indeed, on the nationalist side, elements overlapped with the Sanbabilini (local right-wing group).

While Americana was a key part of the look, featuring such branded items as Timberland deck shoes, Vans, Schott leather jackets and Ray-Ban sunglasses, more favoured were lesser-known home-grown brands, including Naj-Oleari underwear, Fiorucci, Moncler, Controvento, Best Company, Stone Island and CP Company, as well as then still-young designer brands such as Armani and Versace. Either way, distinct brands were important – the paninari's badge of cool. Transport from sandwich bar to sandwich bar – notably between branches of the now-defunct Burghy Milanese fast-food chain, which became their secondary hang-outs – was, inevitably, by Lambretta or Vespa scooter. This was one reason why paninari also favoured distinctive, boldly coloured backpacks.

Distinctively for a subculture, the paninari did not make any attempt to keep their movement underground, self-consciously detached from the mainstream or out of public view. Rather, would-be poseurs, they embraced media attention: throughout the 1980s, several Italian magazines, including *Paninaro*, *Wild Boys* and *Preppy*, were published documenting the paninaro culture, while in 1986, the Pet Shop Boys' single 'Paninaro' brought the style more international attention. So well known were the paninari in Italy that TV comedy shows even lampooned their look. ∎

ABOVE: The cover of a 1987 edition of Paninaro, *one of Italy's many magazines dedicated to the paninaro lifestyle and fashion in the 1980s.*

BELOW: This Milanese paninaro in 1987 wears the classic uniform of his style tribe: Moncler puffa jacket (which remained a quintessential garment of Italian youth), designer jeans and Timberland boots.

The Burghy burger chain was one of the preferred hang-outs for the Paninari. Here a group pose in front of the outlet on Milan's San Babila Square.

Sun worship as style

IDEA № 68

RIO BEACH STYLE

In a culture in which fashion and advertising in the West increasingly pushes the idea of the body beautiful, the beach fashion of Rio de Janeiro has been doing this since the 1950s. The Brazilian city's famed beaches, such as Copacabana and Ipanema, have become almost bywords for seaside exoticism – perhaps stemming from the spirit of free living, barely suppressed sexuality, colour and vibrancy that characterized Brazil's wide-reaching Tropicalismo artistic movement of the 1960s.

ABOVE: Perhaps the biggest global impact of Rio Beach style was seen in Havaianas, a Brazilian brand of flip-flop that became the definitive style of the footwear. By 2010 the company was making over 150m pairs a year to meet demand.

Yet dress, however minimal, however much designed to enhance the tan, remains bound by unofficial rules. Men wear swim-trunks or board shorts – never a football shirt, not even that of the national team. For women barely-there bikinis, perhaps in crocheted form, are essential, bathing suits outré; a sarong or 'kanga' doubles as both something to sit on and to wrap up in (nobody uses a towel); a floppy, broad-brimmed hat and maybe a T-shirt, cut down at the sleeves and barely covering the bust, provide some respite from the sun; flip-flops, ideally by local company Havaianas, protect the feet from hot sands.

And it is a look that translates to the streets off the beach and around town, a move made possible both by the climate and by the Brazilian readiness to expose flesh. It transposes less well to European rock and pop festivals, where it was re-created by festival-goers in the late 1990s and early 2000s – the bikini worn with sarong, flip-flops, floppy, broad-brimmed hat and outsized sunglasses. ∎

The mother of all festivals, Woodstock, in Bethel, New York, in 1969 – in keeping with the hippy era, festival-goers take a more earthy approach to dress, dispensing with footwear altogether to take on the mud.

The catwalk of mud

IDEA № 69

FESTIVAL FASHION

The rebirth of the music festival scene in the UK from the late 1990s onwards – after its 1970s heyday and following in the wake of the enduring Glastonbury Festival in southwest England – gave muddy fields and plastic cups a whole new fashionability with the youth market.

Festivals, of course, had long been a focal point for moments in fashion – in the case of hippie style for example, and its defining event, Woodstock; **bohemian** style similarly saw festivals as its catwalk. But, by the 1990s, with the revival of the festival as a popular format for live music, especially across Europe, practical concerns of camping and inclement weather butted up against the need to look as on-trend as the latest bands and certainly as fellow festival-goers – consequently a new festival-going uniform for women developed. Key elements of this look included Hunter wellington boots, vests, micro-shorts or denim cut-offs (sometimes worn over tights, and with pocket bags revealing themselves below the hem), big belts, big hats, ethnic jewellery, shoulder bags and, ideally, plastic 'VIP access only' bracelets.

British supermodel Kate Moss pioneered the style, one slavishly copied by fast-fashion retailers. The look, appropriately, was essentially that of the 1970s groupie or rock chick with practical touches (the wellington boots, for example, which would subsequently find new fashionability on the streets and a long way from any mud). Checked shirts, parkas, floral prints and accessories, band T-shirts and cowboy boots might add a boho touch.

Other festival-goers saw the big party as a chance to open the dressing-up box, mixing together club-night paraphernalia such as tutus, angel's wings, tinsel and neon accessories – the stuff of the club night worn out in broad daylight. ∎

ABOVE: *Two festival-goers at Hultsfield Festival, Sweden, in 2006, epitomizing the Kate Moss-inspired festival style that followed the explosion of renewed interest in the festival scene in the early 21st century: outsize sunglasses, vest tops, denim cut-offs (ideally showing the bottom of the pocket bags) and wellington or cowboys boots.*

BELOW: *Festival fashion must be ready to deal with inclement weather and, given the mass of people on the move around open fields, inevitably much mud, as these festival-goers are facing at Glastonbury Festival, at Worthy Farm in Pilton, UK, in 2011.*

A new kind of statement dressing

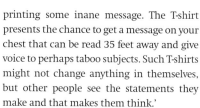

IDEA Nº 70

PROTEST CLOTHING

So cheap did the plain T-shirt become by the 1980s that it spawned a DIY approach to what could be on its front – allowing people not only to custom-make their own, but to give almost immediate voice to their opinion of current affairs. When LAPD police officers were acquitted for the beating of Rodney King in 1992, T-shirts condemning the court's decision appeared within a few hours.

The T-shirt's blank canvas has consequently been a site to protest about or to raise awareness on all sorts of issues: civil and gay rights, anti-apartheid, anti-globalization, from campaigning against nuclear weapons or for greater environmental awareness to matters of philosophy and health. Indeed, since the 1960s – with marches against Vietnam in the US – T-shirts have been scrawled on or printed with phrases and logos that have made them 'sandwich boards' expressing a multitude of viewpoints. Movements of all kinds continue to use the T-shirt in this way.

Fashion's embrace of the protest t-shirt, however, came in the 1980s, when British fashion designer Katharine Hamnett designed a series of outsized T-shirts with large slogans on them, including in 1984 '58% Don't Want Pershing', which she pointedly wore to meet then British prime minister Margaret Thatcher. Other T-shirt statements included 'Worldwide Nuclear Ban Now', 'Education Not Missiles', 'Use a Condom' and 'I Love CSP' (concentrated solar power), and Hamnett's intention was that people should copy her T-shirts and thereby disseminate the messages.

However, with the exception of the 'Target' campaign of T-shirts, highlighting the issue of breast cancer, the fashion industry has largely avoided controversy. Indeed, Hamnett has gone on record stating her annoyance at other designers reviving the look of her T-shirts but then 'just printing some inane message. The T-shirt presents the chance to get a message on your chest that can be read 35 feet away and give voice to perhaps taboo subjects. Such T-shirts might not change anything in themselves, but other people see the statements they make and that makes them think.'

It has been left to radicalized individuals and more underground brands, notably those for the skateboarding and streetwear communities, to take the idea of protest clothing further, most notably by tampering with corporate logos. So called 'brandalism' aims to undercut the logo's original meaning. Some go on to become underground bestsellers, for example the advertising slogan 'Enjoy Coca-Cola' rewritten as 'Enjoy Cocaine', and the brand 'Adidas' as 'Adihash'. Others, such as those by Rick Klotz, founder of casualwear brand Freshjive, are more subtle, re-working corporate logos – the likes of that of the Seven-Eleven convenience store chain, or the graphic style of washing powder packaging – in **T-Shirt graphics** to make some kind of political commentary. The Holiday Inn logo, for instance, was re-worked to read 'Holiday In Iraq' in 2003. 'I like to use graphics to express my distaste for, ironically perhaps, the commercialism of fashion,' Klotz once noted. ∎

RIGHT: *Fashion designer Katharine Hamnett can take credit for re-invigorating the T-shirt as a canvas for protest from 1983, even helping to turn it into a kind of fashion item.*

OPPOSITE: *The logo of the Campaign for Nuclear Disarmament is worn by two women in 1970. Similar T-shirts would be seen a decade later, in 1981, at the long-lived Greenham Common women's protest camp in the UK, established in protest against the siting of American nuclear cruise missiles on UK soil.*

Godfather of Grunge, Seattle band
Nirvana's frontman Kurt Cobain
made a signature of patched jeans
and sloppy, outsized sweaters.

Thriftiness as style

IDEA № 71
GRUNGE

If charity-shop clothing had become its own kind of fashion by the twenty-first century, it was grunge that pioneered the idea that a certain style could be born of thriftiness. While grunge was primarily a music genre, its participants' perhaps self-conscious disregard for fashion (to pursue style might be to undermine the integrity of the music) ironically came to define a fashion, albeit one assembled on the cheap.

ABOVE: *Actress Bridget Fonda in Cameron Crowe's romantic comedy* Singles *(1992), which capitalized on the interest in the Seattle grunge scene by using it as a backdrop for the plot. The Fonda character's kooky found-garment style – bowler-style hat, biker jacket, print dress – captured grunge's mix and don't-match aesthetic.*

LEFT: *Model Christy Turlington models designer Marc Jacobs's grunge-inspired collection for Perry Ellis in 1993, when the street trickled up to the catwalk.*

Ripped, grubby denims, graphic T-shirts, heavy flannel checked overshirts, baggy sweaters and cardigans, basic pumps, combat boots or Dr. Martens shoes (which experienced a sales boom off the back of grunge), with obligatory lank hair under beanie hats – not too dissimilar from the dishevelled, unwashed look of the Generation X American teenager, in other words – comprised a look that was accessible, affordable and easy. It was an anti-fashion fashion.

Grunge was a term applied to the music coming out of (chiefly) the United States's Pacific Northwest during the late 1980s and early 1990s, driven by bands such as Sonic Youth, Pearl Jam, Hole, Soundgarden, Dinosaur Jr. and, most famously, Nirvana. It suggested angst, energy, nihilism and a certain anti-establishment disenchantment of the kind previously embodied by punk, and, with its feedback and distortion in a raw, guitar-driven wall of sound, was described – by Mudhoney's lead singer Mark Arm – as 'pure noise'. The clothing worn by the bands was arguably a sartorial expression of the same: a determination not to buy into the glamour or consumerism of the 'designer decade', to subvert particular dress codes or sartorial expectations: 'pure clothing', as it were, with functionality – covering up, keeping warm and comfortable – first and last.

Inevitably perhaps, thanks to the interest of fashion media and manufacturers, grunge style became precisely what it never was – a high-profile fashion trend (in fact, many of the bands even expressed a discomfort at the music itself becoming as big as it did). For spring/summer 1993 Marc Jacobs, then designer for fashion label Perry Ellis, created a collection based on the look but this time in luxury fabrics and with hefty price tags. It won Jacobs the Council for Fashion Designers of America's Designer of the Year award. ∎

From street to catwalk

BELOW: *Styles that originated on the street have long influenced those presented on the catwalks, as here, with a punk girl on the Kings Road in London, in 1984, and in tamer form as part of the Abbey Dawn by Avril Lavigne spring/summer 2013 collection.*

OPPOSITE: *Hipster style also interacts between the street and high fashion versions, here embodied by a couple on London's Brick Lane and the runway take by designer Yanuk.*

IDEA № 72
TRICKLE-UP

The oldest and most accepted theory as to the way fashion works is that the wealthier upper ranks of society set the trends for the masses; or, in more contemporary terms, the most exclusive fashion companies set the styles through catwalk shows, which are then emulated on the street in a form both more affordable and less extreme. This is the so-called trickle-down theory.

But from the 1960s, and especially in the 1980s, that idea began to be challenged. It seemed that the dominant idea of fashion's function was better expressed by the complete reverse of this, trickle-up, whereby it is with the less well-off classes, and more specifically through their creative subcultures, that new ways of dressing are developed, these only gaining mainstream approval when the wealthier classes have adopted them and made them their own. (A third theory, 'trickle-across', suggests that, thanks to mass media, trends move horizontally through groups of the same social standing, age, taste or market, with style leaders within a given group setting trends and influencing peers, leading to multiple simultaneous fashion trends around the world.)

Trickle-up suggests that, while fashion design companies have the freedom to refine an idea and the financial and communications heft to popularize it, the real creativity lies with an individual and how he or she chooses to wear something. Certainly designer fashions have reflected a closer attention to streetwear innovations since the post-World War II consumer booms that empowered average people to dress as they chose. Just as Coco Chanel suggested that the style of the well-to-do originated in working-class dress sense, recent decades have also seen examples of trickle-up such as punk, grunge, 'gypsy' style, military surplus as fashion, as well as more focused trends, such as nail art. Some fashion theorists have argued that fashion's direction is a reflection of the status of youth: when the median age of a society is older, trickle-down dominates; when it is younger, trickle-up rules. ■

'Real creativity lies with an individual and how he or she chooses to wear something.'

Tripping out, dressing up

IDEA № 73
RAVE

Its cartoon excesses have since often seen the look of the rave years ridiculed. But in its freedom of expression and its creative dressing up for all-night, often drug-fuelled dance sessions, rave culture defined its own style outside of the mainstream.

The rave scene in Britain ran loosely from 1987, when the first ecstasy seizures were reported and when Steve 'Silk' Hurley had the first house music number one in the UK with 'Jack Your Body', to 1993, when the British government clamped down on it with the 'rave clause' of its Criminal Justice Act. Much of the ravers' style was practical, including T-shirts to deal with the heat of clubland (especially key in its spiritual home of Ibiza) and bumbags in which to hold one's personal effects (and personal supply). Much of the clothing and accessories favoured white or bright neons, to catch the clubs' fluorescent UV or laser lights. Graphics were a form both of shared identity and, in a sense, of the shared philosophy that came from a 'belief' in the community-spiritedness of ecstacy use – they were irreverent ('Drop acid, not bombs'), jokey and sometimes iconic, most notably the acid house 'Smiley' (first used for a flyer for the pioneering Shoom club night in 1988 and soon spawning an anti-drugs version with a down-turned mouth).

But other choices were more eccentric: boiler suits and gloves, baby's dummies, leg and arm warmers, tie-dyed and other hippyish paraphernalia, bandanas, novelty sunglasses, the essential glow-sticks and whistles and, in the north of England, where 'Madchester' had created its own rival rave variant, page-boy haircuts, Kickers shoes and huge flares. None of it was too subtle as you tried to make your way to an illegal countryside event, the location of which was revealed only an hour or so before via pre-cell-phone messaging services. Rave was, essentially, a hedonistic, style-less environment; clothes were about fun, about 'anything goes', an approach that was reflected in the clubs themselves on occasion. In 1998 DJ and rave-night host Paul Oakenfold plunged his Spectrum club, London, into darkness while playing Tchaikovsky's *1812 Overture*. ∎

ABOVE: *Clubbers at Spectrum, Jubilee Gardens, in London in 1988, the headband and loose-fit T-shirts especially linking them stylistically to the so-called Manchester/Madchester 'baggy' scene of the same period.*

LEFT: *A nu rave night in London in 2006 demonstrates both the longevity of rave but also the change in style towards the more brash, colourful and, at times, cartoony.*

Sameness in difference

BELOW: *British indie band The Charlatans in Wales in the 1990s. Their style typified the indie look, most notably in their regard for old school/casual Adidas sneakers – the likes of the Gazelle and Campus – and anoraks, which in any other context might be considered nerdish. Invariably these were worn fastened to the neck, regardless of weather.*

OPPOSITE: *Like the Charlatans, the fashion sensibility of the British indie band Blur in its early years, had an influence on mainstream street style. Indeed, after the pomp of the 1980s, the 1990s saw pop and rock stars dress increasingly like their audience.*

IDEA № 74
INDIE KID STYLE

When in the mid-1990s, all things independent – stores, music, media, film – were celebrated for their break with a growing homogeneity, street fashion was not left out. Indie fashion followed an independent mindset, with artistically inclined teens and twenty-somethings seeking to carve an alternative, more individualistic path away from major trends and, for some, away from consumerism.

One way this suggestion of the anti-consumerist was expressed was through the indie kids' regard for the hand-made – less in the sense of bespoke as those items made by individuals and bought at craft fairs rather than in shops. The cottage industry this suggested was the right side of capitalism.

Indie style was more considered than grunge, less scene-making than **hipster**,

without the piercings or stylized hair and make-up of **emo**, although related to all three. Indie was characterized by the wearing of a mix of the second-hand, distressed and beaten, dandyish, down-home and, often, modified through cutting and dyeing – especially if this allowed the individualiZing of a mass-market garment. Items included waistcoats and plaid flannel shirts,

fedoras and beanies, drainpipe jeans, Converse sneakers and other cheap canvas plimsolls, tweed jackets, skinny neckties, slouchy cardigans, short floral-print dresses, vintage jewellery, army surplus coats, hoodies and brand logo-free printed T-shirts. It was a pick-and-mix of retro and contemporary references and styles, coherent only in the way they were styled together and in being apart from other more identifiable subcultures.

As such, it shared the 'indie' label with both music (especially in the UK with Britpop during the 1990s) and film-making. In these fields, the term also suggested a distinction from the more corporate mainstream and perhaps more avant-garde credentials. And the wearing of T-shirts bearing the names of indie bands – the only acceptable face of branding – certainly became part of the indie fashion uniform.

Ultimately, indie kids, through their clothing, actively sought to distance themselves from any scene, to the point where they would inevitably not choose to label themselves indie kids. The problem, perhaps, was that in doing so, they became a scene by default. Indie became an identifiable style of dress. ∎

Anti-fashion fashion

IDEA № 75
GEEK CHIC

Buddy Holly had tried contact lenses – in the early 1950s, a new invention – but he found them unbearable within minutes. Eventually he conceded that, even as a pop star, he would have to wear glasses. And Holly's Texas optometrist, Dr J. David Armstead, did not offer him anything subtle.

Armstead had picked up two pairs of extra-thick Faiosa frames while travelling in Mexico and persuaded Holly to wear the black, as opposed to the more subtle tortoise-shell, pair. Holly agreed, although for his first few performances he refused to wear them, effectively going on stage blind. His manager, smartly, insisted he wear them – not only to avoid potential accidents, but also because he saw in the look something different. So-called geek chic was born.

Indeed, if the stereotypical association of glasses with unmanly bookish intellectualism was by then well established, Holly gave them a new Clark Kent cool too, one

that would both last and become a style in its own right. Teamed with clothes deemed permanently unfashionable, such as tan tops, braces, bow-ties, clumpy shoes, T-shirts with captions, ill-fitting tailoring, and in some instances glossed with irony, the anti-fashion style of the geek – or even the more indie-style inspired geekette – would become a new fashion archetype. Expressing one's smarts became smart.

It was a look, from the 1990s on, that was embraced by celebrities, Justin Timberlake, Johnny Depp, Justin Bieber and David Beckham among them; by designers, including CFDA Menswear Designer of the Year Thom Browne, with his influential Peewee Herman-inspired 'shrunken' suit style of ankle-skimming trousers and short, boxy jackets; and perhaps even by new cultural heroes, from Apple's Steve Jobs to Facebook's Mark Zuckerberg, both of whom helped elevate geekiness via the global importance of the personal computing revolution. At one point it became so fashionable to wear glasses that they would be worn with clear lenses by those with perfect eyesight. Popular culture's post-dotcom celebration of the geek – notably via a newfound respect for science, technology and entrepreneurialism – underlined the style appeal of outward displays of intellectualism, whether real or just suggested. ■

LEFT: In London in 2009 two stylistic choices that had long since been condemned to fashion purdah – the bow-tie and the moustache – were revived. The geeky spectacles added to the anti-fashion fashion.

ABOVE: Well-known for his love of second-hand clothing, especially tailoring from the 1970s, as well as his trademark glasses, Pulp's frontman Jarvis Cocker, here at the Glastonbury Festival, is a hero of geek chic.

OPPOSITE: London's Graduate Fashion Week in 2010 saw geek styling in force: bow-tie, anorak, back-pack.

Digital-age style setters

IDEA № 76
CELEBRITY

Celebrities have long had a close relationship with fashion. Fashion designers dressed them for film roles and red carpet events alike, in some cases building ties that made star and style inseparable, as with Audrey Hepburn and Givenchy, for example. Celebrity-specific press has existed in parallel to report what celebrities wear.

But with the late 1990s' advent of the internet and the mid-2000s' development of social media (both in its ability to rapidly disseminate imagery and its use by celebrities as a means of branding), the reporting of how celebrities dressed for their private lives increased exponentially, and with it their power to shape street trends. It was one that arguably trumped that of catwalk fashions and fast-fashion retailers alike.

Certainly several of the key womenswear trends of the 2000s were initiated by celebrities (and/or their professional stylists): actresses Michelle Williams and Zooey Deschanel shaped hipster, while Mary-Kate and Ashley Olsen and Lindsay Lohan, among others, shaped boho. Even specific items could become street fashion trends off unofficial celebrity endorsement: Gwen Stefani and Britney Spears popularized tube tops and bare midriffs, Madonna is said to have prompted a trend for velour tracksuits, Jessica Simpson for Ugg boots.

Certain celebrities were able to parlay that influence into the building of successful fashion brands under their own names, including the Olsen sisters, who launched a line for Walmart; Simpson, with her Jessica Simpson Collection; Stefani ,with her L.A.M.B. line; as well as singers Victoria Beckham, Justin Timberlake, Robbie Williams and Liam Gallagher, among others (with many hip hop stars also having a major sideline in clothing). Many were multi-million- and in some cases even billion-dollar enterprises. Other celebrities lent their names to lines designed for established fashion companies, while still others became the face of certain brands – an inversion of the clichéd model-turned-actor career path. ∎

LEFT: *High-street brands the likes of H&M was among the many through the 1990s and early 2000s to tap into the profile of celebrity in order to sell clothing – an H&M hoarding in London in 2007 here plugs a collection designed by 'Maj', aka Madonna.*

ABOVE: *Gwen Stefani was one of the earliest celebrities to launch her own clothing line, L.A.M.B, and make a success of it. Here the pop star poses with the Harajuku Girls (Stefani's dance troupe) at the 32nd Annual American Music Awards in Los Angeles.*

OPPOSITE: *A cheeky advertisement, given its huge dimensions, for the David Beckham underwear line, covering a 34th Street building in Manhattan, New York in 2012.*

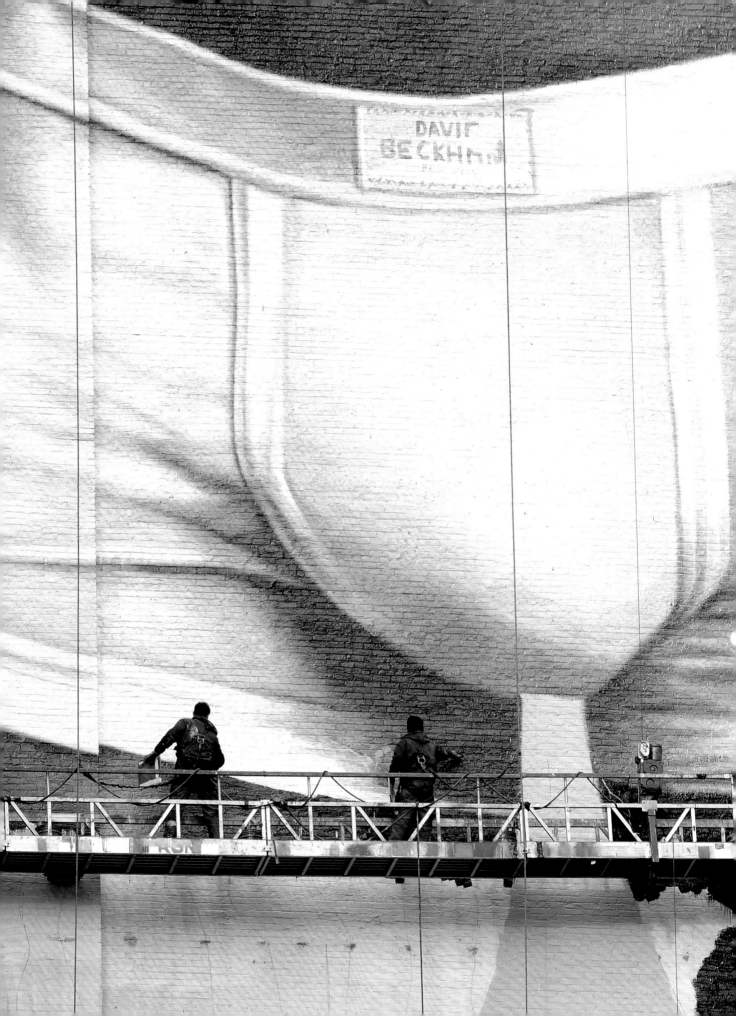

Dayglo and darkness

TECHNO

Glow-sticks and baby's dummies might not be the most auspicious of beginnings for a style with a future – but it was precisely with one eye on tomorrow that many of the tropes of the look that accompanied techno music were established.

Techno was a heavily syncopated, looped drum, bass and hi-hat-based sound that originated in Detroit as a post-disco genre in the mid-1980s, giving birth to various musical subgenres. Closely related to the look of cyberpunks, the dress of followers of techno reflected the forward-looking drive of the music, spreading from Detroit, and really finding its expression in clothing by the time it had caught hold abroad, notably in Japan and Germany – the home, after all, of electronic music.

That futuristic quality stemmed, in part, from its break with the past – a consequence of its largely cutting-edge electronic instrumentation, which, according to techno pioneer Derrick May, appealed because it

was 'classy and clean, beautiful like outer space', a contrast to Detroit where 'everything is an ugly mess'. This futurism was later underlined by the music's association with the latest drugs – most notably at the time ecstacy – and by it coming, for some, to be the music of anti-capitalist angst.

Indeed, techno dress existed in its clubland bubble – a means of shared self-identification for its fan-base, akin, perhaps, to that of northern soul in the UK – and rarely found itself copied as fashion outside it, with the exception perhaps of a few conceptual designers working outside the fashion mainstream. And given the dystopian, Clockwork Orange-esque theatricality of much of it, that is perhaps not surprising. The look embraced overtly synthetic fabrics in eye-searingly vibrant colours, part-childish, part-fetishistic, part-alien Day-Glo accessories, towering platform sneakers, gas masks, brightly dyed hair, camouflage (preferably in bright colours rather than the standard greens and browns) and other, often customized industrial work clothing, from hi-vis jackets and trousers to anti-radiation suits. ∎

ABOVE: The more industrial, apocalyptic style of techno was suggested by the wearing of boiler suits and, here, air filter masks, at a club in Milton Keynes, UK.

OPPOSITE: A woman on Berlin's Love Parade in 2003 – the name of the event suggesting the somewhat softer side to the techno scene.

'The dress of followers of techno reflected the forward-looking drive of the music.'

The longing for difference

IDEA Nº 78
THE HIPSTER

Twenty-somethings desperate to be alternative, obsessed with rediscovering the past, customizing their own second-hand clothes rather than wearing the latest fashions, determined that everything they do, have and wear be authentic, even ironically so, and measuring an item's appeal by how cool it is – these were the chief characteristics of a hipster.

The term derives from the 1940s American jazz scene, when hipsters and hep-cats – from the street slang of 'hip' and 'hep', denoting the underground and progressive – were the nattily dressed followers of the jazz and bebop counterculture. In the mid-1990s, and onwards through the first decade of the twenty-first century, however, the contemporary hipster was likely to be found wearing recent vintage – from the 1980s, for example – mixed with appealingly obscure new fashion labels, listening to as-yet unsigned bands and musing over undiscovered artists, ideally those with a street-art bent (knowledge of which was greatly boosted by the growth in internet access).

To the hipster, difference from the mainstream was everything, down to the embracing of the tropes of alternative lifestyle: veganism, anti-consumerism, political liberalism, retro affectations and the like. This was also why their main playgrounds were independent coffee shops in the overlooked corners of urban centres wherever regeneration and gentrification were about to happen – the likes of Shibuya in Tokyo, Shoreditch in London, Williamsburg in New York, Kreuzberg in Berlin, and the Marais in Paris.

Indeed, while hipsters shared no defining style, they did share an aesthetic: quirky but not cute; individualistic while also managing to embrace a uniform; blurred gender lines; left-field even if this was of questionable style or taste. They also shared an attitude – a kind of postmodern appropriation of anything outside the mainstream, whether good and bad, the mere selection of which implied a stamp of approval. Non-hipsters would later attempt to adopt certain hipster trends – for outsized prescription glasses (even for those with perfect eyesight), retro and fixed-gear bicycles, trucker caps, neon nail polish, super-skinny jeans and certain haircuts, such as the 'Hoxton fin' (a kind of false mohican or mohawk) – the whole lot accessorized with the latest Apple laptop. Viewing hipster taste as in some way leading edge, both fashion and lifestyle brands would also attempt to co-opt some of these looks. ∎

East London, the city's hipster magnet during the early 2000s, saw the skateboard become an accessory among grown men, even if skate style had long since been considered passé.

Individualist as stylist

IDEA № 79
EXTREME SPORTS

Call them extreme sports – snowboarding, BMXing, paragliding, free-climbing, BASE jumping and parkour, among the many that began multiplying in the 1990s – but they are just as much alternative sports. And with them came an alternative outlook towards language, music and clothing, and a culture that has defined their participants as, above all, progressive individuals.

Indeed, crucially to their romantic appeal, most extreme or alternative sports are individual not team activities. As a consequence, both fashion brands and fashion media, including MTV, were keen to tap into their aesthetic and attitude from the outset (with diverse brands following, from soft drinks to fragrances). And the 'extremists' and especially their star players – some of whom would be signed up to model – had an influence on street style. With extreme sports, for the first time sport and specifically urban fashion blurred in a feedback loop.

Brands launched by extremists, and others launched to service their specific needs – for example Airwalk, No Fear, DC, Oakley and Hang Ten – quickly found crossover appeal with a youth market that might not actually parachute off skyscrapers or board out of helicopters but aspired to the lifestyle such edgy activities suggested. Much as skateboarding helped shape the late twentieth-century generic teen uniform of baggy T-shirt, workwear and skate shoes, so extreme sports in turn created a street-level demand for tough,

technical fabrics and functional products, bright colours and bold patterns, neon and reflectivity, padding and quilting, ostentatious logos and branding. Such was the clothing equivalent of the inner-city trend for 4×4 vehicles that almost never went off-road, but looked the part and gave some satisfaction in offering the capability.

Indeed, part of the appeal of extreme sports in style terms was that each represented the type of closed society that previous, music-driven subcultures such as mod or punk had offered. Now such subcultures were sports-driven and thrived on the buzz of adrenaline rather than drugs. ∎

OPPOSITE TOP: *Parkour, or free-running – leaping over, around and through urban obstacles – required considerable gymnastics and bravery. Here a practitioner makes a move at Waterloo roundabout, London, 2008.*

OPPOSITE BOTTOM: *BMXing, similarly, required an acceptance of spills along with the thrills – BMXer Vinnie Hunter performed a downside foot-plant at a skatepark in the East Midlands, UK.*

RIGHT: *One of the most combative, full contact new sports, mixing the physicality of rugby and ice hockey, is the roller derby, which stylistically often favoured rockabilly and psychobilly touches, from 50s-inspired tattoos to piercings and hairstyles.*

Dial F for fashion

THE CELL PHONE

As the bicycle, motorbike, scooter or low-priced car provided young people with their first independent mobility, so the cell phone became their first private form of round-the-clock communications. And, as cell phones became smartphones around 2007, they also became youth's social media portal, life recorder and occasional creative tool.

A device first popularized for pre-teens and teenagers by parents as a means of tracking their children's movements and ensuring some degree of security (as was the case with the pagers that preceded them) would become a means of circumventing such oversight, connecting its 'always on' user with the networked world through 'moblogging' (mobile blogging) and a continuous link-up to social media. This provided not only the ultimate tool of short-order organization, be it for a party or a riot, but turned the phone into an indispensable tool for sharing ideas, spreading trends and shopping.

What was perhaps less expected was how the ubiquitous phones themselves would become coveted youth status objects too, the teen and twenty-something equivalent of a Swiss watch, 'it' bag or jewellery. Particular manufacturers and models would move in and out of favour like fashion brands, and personal customization through covers and wallpapers became essential. Phone-jacking – mugging for phones – was an inner-city commonplace.

The cell phone as style accessory was available in multiple colours, in special editions, with leather trim or designer brand tie-in – Anna Sui, Prada, Dolce & Gabbana and Versace were just some of the first fashion names put to a specific look of phone – or carried with cell-phone charms attached. Some considered the wearing of a Bluetooth earpiece itself a kind of accessory. A 2007 study of youth in Ukraine found that such was the cell phone's importance as a status object that some would forego the communications benefits of a cell phone in order to avoid having to publicly display an old or 'ugly' model – in other words, they preferred no phone at all than to unfashionable one. ■

ABOVE: *Cell-phone cases, or skins, have become a means of differentiating a mass-market item and making one's phone an expression of one's personality. In this instance, a leopard print skin has been used in Berlin, 2012.*

RIGHT: *A mobile phone can be further personalized by the addition of accessories, such as these keyring-type devices, which light up in response to an incoming phone call. Such accessories were especially big among Japanese teenagers.*

OPPOSITE: *For a brief spell after its launch, the wearing of a Bluetooth earpiece became a fashion in its own right – signalling one's connectivity and, some might say, self-importance.*

Fancy dress as fashion

IDEA № 81
COSPLAY

If Halloween, fancy dress parties and Mardi Gras all invite grown adults to dress up in themed clothes of a kind they would not wear otherwise, cosplay (costume play) revels in dressing up for its own sake. First popularized in the late 1980s, cosplay is somewhat akin to amateur dramatics without the stage, its participants using costumes and accessories to present themselves as a character from a variety of sources.

ABOVE: With a nod to Elvira, Ms Monster became such a cult figure on the cosplay scene that she got her own cable TV show in San Francisco. Here she poses at the Comicon 2008 Comic Convention in San Diego.

OPPOSITE: A cosplayer at the Kapow Comic Convention in London in 2011, the Lycra suit arguably doing him few favours measured against the physiques of more traditional superheroes.

Cosplayers adopt the clothing and sometimes the accent, physical traits and mannerisms of a specific, often idolized character (sometimes even of the opposite sex) from science fiction, fantasy, comic books – both the classic American Marvel and DC variety and the more modern Japanese manga and anime – video games, films or TV series. The result is inevitably much bolder and more outlandish than, for example, historical re-enactment in period dress.

Cosplay has allowed elements to feed into street fashion in those cultures in which more expressive, elaborate dressing was already the basis of distinct fashion (as opposed to hobbyist) subcultures, most notably in Japan. There anime characters became a popular source of inspiration for cosplay: outfits echoing those of anime characters the likes of Gundam Seed, Durarara, Rurouno Kenshin and Burst Angel, among many others, are available commercially. However, the crossover between cosplay as recreation and cosplay as fashion remained much less distinct elsewhere, especially in the West.

It was when video games went mass-market in the 1990s, together with the advent of the internet, which helped cosplayers communicate and share ideas, that cosplay really took off. The admired skill in cosplay, however, remained more analogue than digital. While character outfits became available off the shelf, or could even be made bespoke, most cosplayers created their own outfits. And it was the accuracy with which they did so – right down to the use of hair colour, body paint, temporary tattoos and coloured or special-effect contact lenses – that won accolades from their cosplay community. It was on such detail that cosplay competitions were judged. ∎

Breaking down stereotypes

IDEA Nº 82

METROSEXUAL

Until the 1980s, manliness – as defined by the movie and advertising industries at least – was hairy-chested and testosterone-fuelled; yet by the mid-90s a new archetype had been established. In his twenties or thirties, with a high disposable income, living in a large urban centre, perhaps narcissistic, perhaps simply careful about his presentation, this was the so-called metrosexual.

The metrosexual style made it acceptable for a man to dress and groom well – to the point of using beauty products typically reserved for use by women – to be design-savvy and interior decoration-literate, without the stereotyped assumption that he must be homosexual. Some metropolitan men on the European continent may have long been comfortable with carrying so-called 'man bags' and getting a good haircut, but this was something new. Indeed, the metrosexual was – for straight male society – a pioneer: a new breed of style-aware shopper, whose impact would be to open a floodgate for menswear, gym and male cosmetics and spa treatment industries.

Publications founded on interest in such subjects followed, defining such interests as everyday for subsequent generations (even if older men remained unconvinced). That led to stark changes in behaviour: if in the mid-1980s a reported quarter of American men bought their own clothes, half were doing so by the mid-90s, and almost three-quarters by the early 2000s. By then it was not uncommon for financial institutions such as Deutsche Bank and Inchcape to hire grooming consultants for their executives.

The term 'metrosexual' was British, coined for a national newspaper article in 1994, but took hold when used again in 2002 in the online magazine Salon.com to define British footballer and sarong-wearer David Beckham as the epitome of the type; it spread further when it was taken up by marketing agency Euro RCSG Worldwide. Brad Pitt was cited as Beckham's American equivalent. Arguably the metrosexual would also prove to be the launch pad for the so-called Adonis complex, in which male teens (or younger) are newly fearful of being insufficiently muscle-bound, much as girls have long been pressured by marketing archetypes into losing weight. ∎

At the Bizarre Ball, in the UK in 2010, Zoe Minihane and friend wear outfits made of plastic toys, akin to the Japanese Decora.

Style at the sci-fi interface

IDEA № 83
CYBERPUNK

If steampunk looks to the distant past for a futuristic vision of style, cyberpunk looked only to the future, albeit a largely dystopian one. While there were no fixed lines as to what defined cyberpunk style, the subculture's anxious view of tomorrow's world as a dark and troubled one was reflected in the austere, noirish costume for such films as *Blade Runner* (1982), *RoboCop* (1987) and *The Matrix* (1999).

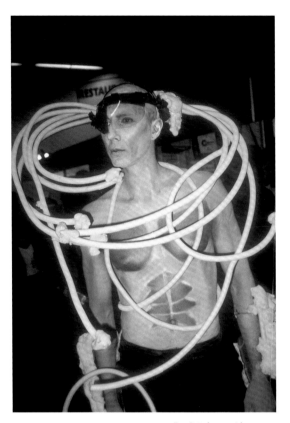

ABOVE: *Zero Luie dresses with cyberpunk's love of the dystopian, here as a cyborg, part body paint, part industrial tubing.*

LEFT: *Goth meets neon: cyberpunks in Santiago, Chile, in 2007*

The style was recognizable as a broad extension of clothing styles today, but with near-future twists in fabrication or cut, and the wearing of 'cyberware' – gadgetry supposedly grafted on to or implanted in the human body. Graphically at its more extreme it was reminiscent of the stagewear of such groups as the 1980s British New Wave band Sigue Sigue Sputnik, whose use of bold colours, fluorescence, extreme shapes and primitive-futurist hairstyles gave more than a nod to the movie genre that included *Mad Max* (1979) and *The Terminator* (1984). Unlike **steampunk** cyberpunk style avoids obvious historic references in order to be forward-looking with conviction: the result was a blend of the tribal (tattoos, braided and shaved hair), the exaggerated (platform boots, skintight, man-made fabrics) and the imagined technological (goggles, air-filtering masks).

A love of the industrial synthetic, from rubber to plastic to any fabric with a surface effect, also informed the look. *Blade Runner* actually predates the 1983 short story by Bruce Bethke, whose title was the first known use of the term 'cyberpunk', as well as predating influential novels of the new genre by K.W. Jeter and William Gibson, whose novels *Dr. Adder* and *Neuromancer* respectively were both published in 1984. In the late 1980s and early 1990s, cyberpunk's peak (although the look spilled over in clubbing scenes for the rest of the decade, especially through the brighter, mangaesque cybergoth spin-off), the disquieting anxieties expressed in the genre's artistic works were that much more real, dealing as they did with such themes as runaway technology and corporatism, breakdown in social order, and globalization. And many of cyberpunk's science fiction near-future concerns continue to exist today, notably philosophical questions related to artificial intelligence and humanity's relationship to it. ∎

Although anti-drink and -drugs, Straight Edgers did not reject all things mainstream society deems subversive: tattoos, for example, remained at the core of Straight Edge's expression of their atypical way of life.

Clothes for a shared ideology

STRAIGHT EDGE

If teen life since the 1950s has, according to the stereotype, been about bucking convention, kicking against authority and searching for hedonistic experiences, perhaps it is hard to explain the rise, during the 1980s, of straight edge. This was a spin-off of the American punk scene which advocated abstinence in all those things that youth is most curious about: sex, drugs and perhaps not rock and roll, but in some instances even meat, caffeine, dairy products and prescription drugs.

BELOW: Seminal straight edge band Minor Threat, performing at the Wilson Center in Washington DC in 1983, with all the raw energy of the movement's philosophical opposite, punk.

ABOVE: Straight-Edgers in the mosh pit at an Evil Fest gig in Camden, London.

Arising first in Washington D.C. and Boston and then spreading across North America, the straight edge lifestyle would also find followers in Europe and the Middle East, despite its quirky, self-imposed outsider status.

Straight edge was the temperance movement revisited by late twentieth-century teenagers, motivated by a combination of a reaction against punk's excesses and nihilism, New Age thinking and sometimes religious conviction. In offering an alternative to what might have seemed to many teens to be the only, potentially self-destructive lifestyle road, arguably straight edge was genuinely revolutionary – the traditional parental message to teens made cool and delivered aggressively.

It also brought about some potentially comic moments, such as when in 1980 pioneering straight edge band Teen Idles was barred admittance to Mabuhay Gardens in San Francisco, where the band was due to play, because all of its members were under the legal age to drink alcohol, which, of course, none did. The incident gave rise to the movement's X logo, after the band members had the backs of their hands marked with a cross to prevent bar staff serving them. That logo would go on to appear on countless T-shirts – as bold a personal statement as, for example, the countercultural T-shirt graphics subverting corporatism from the late 1980s, or the T-shirts with more direct political sloganeering also favoured by straight edgers.

Indeed, straight edge may have been a lifestyle before it was a style, but its followers shared their convictions by sharing a unisex, hardcore skater-inspired look: black or dark distressed clothing was favoured, loose-fit worker trousers or jeans (quite deliberately preferred to avoid potential confusion with emo kids in their skinny jeans), long wallet chains and black combat boots. Seemingly at odds with the clean-living ethos, tattoos were also enthusiastically embraced, some expressing the straight edge philosophy or denoting a lifelong commitment to it, others denouncing those in thrall to alcohol or drugs. The X was a particularly key choice of tattoo, sometimes being proudly displayed on the back of a hand (or other typically exposed parts of the body, such as the neck) as a permanent reminder not to stray from the path back to the excesses many previously knew. ∎

Repackaging the past

IDEA № 85
RETRO

Some items of clothing, or ways of wearing them, are so intimately connected with a specific period of history that, deliberately or otherwise, they cannot help but look out of sync with modern times: floral dresses, for example, are inherently 1940s, black leather biker jackets 1950s, psychedelic prints 1960s, bell-bottom jeans 1970s.

The more time has passed between the original period and the current time, the easier the identification of these items becomes, and the more they become embedded in the public imagination as belonging to a certain period (even if the factual accuracy of this may sometimes be considerably off). The wearing of them becomes retro.

The term was first used in relation to fashion in France, following the 'mode rétro' of the 1970s, in which the behaviour of French civilians during the German occupation of World War II was reassessed in French novels and cinema; the term was then applied to French fashion that recalled the period. 'Retro' was soon more widely adopted by the media in the UK, somewhat pejoratively, to identify this new regard for specifically wartime fashions. After the fashion progressiveness of the 1960s, this, indeed, seemed especially retrograde.

If fashion almost always seeks to reinvent the past – perhaps most clothing has something retro in it – then retro also pointed to the industry's newfound readiness to quickly revive what was barely out of fashion for a new, younger audience, much as the mid-2000s saw a 1990s retro fashion.

From the 1990s onwards, retro fashion became a style in its own right, sometimes accused of being more akin to costume, sometimes of being purely nostalgic for a time its wearers never knew and could not understand. Such events as the UK's Goodwood Revival (which celebrates road-racing cars and motorbikes from the motor sports of the 1950s and 1960s) and other festivals became focal points for retro fashion fans, most often with leanings towards the 1940s; Japanese men's youth culture has been especially enamoured of the 1950s; while the American hit TV series *Mad Men* inspired an early 1960s retro revival. Each period is embraced for the brief time that it is back in fashion. ■

OPPOSITE TOP: *Vintage style would, for some, be as much a lifestyle as a way of dress. Key events on the calendar became an opportunity to step back in time and mingle with those who similarly appreciated the rose-tinted glamour of a past decade. Here, a guest at the Goodwood Revival, UK, wears a tweed three-piece suit despite the summer sunshine.*

OPPOSITE BOTTOM: *London's Jitterbug Ball, with its World War Two-themed setting.*

RIGHT: *Tommi, a young woman who favours 1970s vintage fashion, shot in Southend, UK, in 2006.*

Goth with added feelings

IDEA Nº 86
EMO

Take the teen stereotype (withdrawn, moody, angst-ridden, antisocial, perhaps self-destructive), give it a soundtrack (melodic, romantic, dramatic rock with fatalistic or confessional lyrics written from a strongly male perspective) and a gently gender-bending, anti-conservative style, and the result is emo.

Dyed black hair, worn with a fringe; dark, distressed clothing; traditional gothic rock iconography, the likes of skulls and studs – emo has a distinctive look the world over. Here are two examples from, above, Santiago, Chile, in 2007, and, below, Mexico, in 2011.

OPPOSITE: *Like goths, emos have faced discrimination and even assault for the way they dress. This emo, the teenage Mexican Armando Valez, prefers to travel with other emos and spend time in more tolerant big cities.*

The term – from 'emotional hardcore', 'emocore' or 'emotional-oriented rock' – was first used in the mid-1980s to describe an offshoot genre of American punk, despite few people on the scene at the time finding it anything but pejorative. It was not until the 1990s that emo bands such as Jimmy Eat World, the Promise Ring, My Chemical Romance, Weezer and Mineral made the emo sensibility a teen staple and emo a recognized if alternative genre – the antithesis to the braggadocio and materialism of hip hop.

For its young fans, the idea, as with most subcultures, was to be alternative in their

dress too, at first in embracing second-hand and vintage clothing – an idea from which emo bedfellow grunge arguably took its cue – then through a signature dark, slim-fitting silhouette. If hip hop was baggy, emo kept its uniform close to the skin; if **goth** was theatrical, emo took much of the darkness but wore it in a modern way. Rightly or wrongly, the association with cultishly depressive youth remained, however; at one point the Russian government even sought to ban emo style (a 'dangerous teen trend') in schools.

Certainly the impact of emo in fashion terms was not insignificant. It helped to make teen male fashion more feminine than it had been before. Hair became a major statement: while the idea that hair must be black (or black with a colour streak) was a key aspect of early emo style, what remained was a spiky, seemingly haphazard flat-ironed and side-parted style with perhaps a swoosh of hair over one eye, all the better to hide behind. And while make-up for men was not uncommon in the rock-and-roll world, emo made it more acceptable for the average teen boy to wear a touch of eyeliner. Indeed, the typical emo uniform comprised the tight black shirt and punkish school tie or short-sleeved black band T-shirt and brightly coloured skinny-fit jeans – before skinny-fit had become a standard for the denim industry and fashion at large. Piercing, especially that of the lip, also entered the mainstream through emo. ■

'If hip hop was baggy, emo kept its uniform close
to the skin; if goth was theatrical, emo took much
of the darkness but wore it in a modern way.'

Trends go into hyperdrive

FAST FASHION

After the late 1990s perhaps no single idea would define street-level fashion as distinctly as fast fashion. The industry saw a leap in design, logistics, supply-chain management, and printing and manufacturing technologies that allowed a company to quickly make an affordable 'copy' of (or piece 'inspired by') designer catwalk fashions the moment they were revealed. As a result, high-street versions of high-fashion styles became available long before the originals.

Indeed, this advance not only reversed the fashion industry's emphasis from top end to mass market – since a given designer look was essentially over by the time it was available to buy – but also helped dramatically shift it away from the traditional biannual fashion seasons and their attendant new trends. Faster fashion gave rise to faster consumption. Consumers developed both an attitude that considered their clothing almost as disposable and a sensibility that demanded monthly, sometimes almost weekly, shifts in trends. Major retailers from around the world, including Urban Outfitters and Gap from the United States, Uniqlo from Japan, Zara from Spain, H&M from Sweden and Topshop from the UK, were only too happy to provide these, since inevitably they generated more footfall and sales. Low prices fostered the speeded-up cycles, though these were achieved principally through manufacturing in developing countries, and were also counter to the more general call for greater sustainability and responsibility.

Arguably the advent of fast fashion also homogenized it. Not only high fashion but also street trends became easily assimilated by the new production and distribution methods, allowing for what was once a niche or underground style culture to go overground at the flick of a factory line switch. And while designer brands may have grown increasingly litigious over high-street copies, no such recourse is available to the pioneers of a street-level look: in being copied, it merely loses its appeal. Indeed, by the early 2000s the symbiosis between catwalk and high street seemed to have been acknowledged by both sides, with the advent of special collections by designers of cachet for the high-street companies – H&M most notably – among them those by the likes of Karl Lagerfeld, Stella McCartney and Martin Margiela. ∎

ABOVE: *Fast fashion's emphasis on affordable clothing often in limited runs has prompted scenes of long queues and mad crushes– such as here at Primark's flagship store in Marble Arch, London – around the world.*

OPPOSITE AND RIGHT: *The opening of the first branches of the chains Top Shop and Zara in Australia.*

Kinkiness as fashion

RIGHT: *Musician Marilyn Manson and striptease artist Dita Von Teese arrive at the Kerrang awards, in London. Their high-gloss, PVC clothes are made by the House of Harlot.*

IDEA № 88
FETISH

Almost by definition it is hard to divorce fetish wear from sex. Many of the subculture's garments find their origins in those designed explicitly for erotic or perhaps underground purposes – for behind bedroom doors, where for some fans they remain. Yet in their being appropriated for club nights and gatherings for fantasy role play, they have been given a second life. The connotations of the subversively sexual remain, and that is a large part of their exhibitionist appeal: skintight leather and high high-heels, 'kinky boots' and catsuits, PVC and peep-hole cut-outs, masks and whips…

Fetishism, of course, is an innately primitive impulse and many of its more recognizable garments date to the eighteenth century or before. Indeed, it has been around for long enough that the wearing of skintight synthetic clothing – spandex, nylon, PVC, latex and rubber – and of black leather, bondage gear, such lingerie as stockings, corsets, bustiers and garters, and high stiletto heels, has become a clichéd shorthand for outré erotic or 'kinky' dressing, sometimes verging on self-parody. It is the stuff of the French maid, sex slave or dominatrix.

It is this supposedly shocking or risqué nature, underlined in some quarters with the addition of Nazi-inflected accessories, much as greasers wore and for a similar purpose – that has made elements of fetish wear appealing to combative subcultures such as punk and goth. It has also worked as striking stagewear for a number of rock and pop groups, the Village People (who, with their Tom of Finland-type handlebar-moustached leather biker character, played on fetishism's place in gay iconography), the Who, the Rolling Stones and Frankie Goes to Hollywood among them; and in the fashion trend of underwear as outerwear. A number of style elements of the fashion were, worn in isolation, deemed acceptable in mainstream fashion – stilettos, corsets, catsuits, leather trousers, and so on.

Certainly, much interest in fetish wear remains specialist, and perhaps always has been: pioneering fetish-wear designer John Sutcliffe's *AtomAge* clothing catalogue was launched in 1965 off the back of a company that made 'weatherproofs for lady pillion riders' but found that much of the leather and vinyl clothing was worn more in private than for protection on the road. One of his more famous designs was the AtomAge Boot Suit, an all-in-one shiny black PVC jumpsuit that incorporated high heels. Niche designers have since provided ever more extravagant styles – although fetish wear's blurring with the mainstream advanced considerably from the early 1980s. While some of its exponents remained genuinely interested in exploring new, unconventional ideas of sexuality, fetish club nights, magazines and fashion made dabbling in fetish wear widely accessible to those who saw it more as titillating or extravagant fun. ■

ABOVE: *Fetish wear became one of the style cues behind punk, as pioneered by designer Vivienne Westwood, and here modelled in her 'Sex' shop on London's Kings Road in 1976. At that time the obvious sexual reference of fetish clothing still had a power to shock a conservative society.*

OPPOSITE: *Latex specialist Atsuko Kudo is just one designer who has taken inspiration from the gaudy, man-made and typically skintight materials associated with mainstream fetish wear, although here the designer uses them in a way that is unexpectedly demure, with a nod to womenswear of the 1940s.*

TAVI GEVINSON'S BLOG

16.9.12

IS THIS THE REAL LIFE? IS THIS JUST FANTASY?

WELL HI.

We have a lot to catch up on. I guess I've put off writing this because there is SO MUCH.

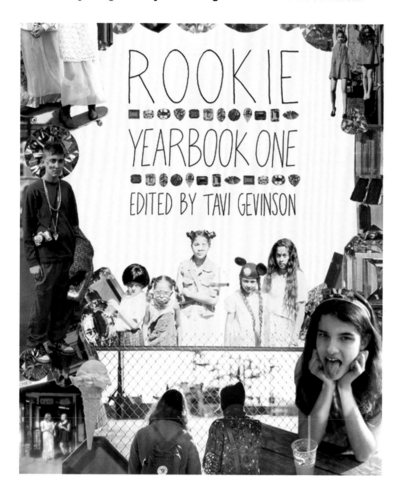

It was always in the back of our minds that we* would do a yearly print edition of *Rookie*, and by the time May rolled around, we realized that we should probably get on that if we wanted to publish it in time for our September anniversary. After a call with Drawn & Quarterly (and years of admiring basically everything they publish), it was clear that they were the perfect publisher for this...book? magazine? of *online content*, edited by a *minor*. IT IS SO AMAZING THAT THEY BELIEVED IN US. I cannot think of better hands to have been in.

In early June, I spent the summer days I had at home living out the PG version of *Dazed and Confused* and working on the book. In late June, the Rookie Road Trip kicked off in New York. We went record shopping and banner-making in Philadelphia, got ice cream in Columbus, played arcade games in Ann Arbor, made zines and saw Girls Rock! Chicago in Chicago (and my WORLDS COLLIDED through a viewing of *Superbad* with my school friends and Rookie staffers), went vintage shopping in Iowa City, saw *Moonrise Kingdom* and crafted at Urban Outfitters in Omaha, raced go-karts in

ABOUT

I write about things that I like. I'm also the founder and editor-in-chief of Rookie. Click through for FAQ.

THE WEBSITE FOR TEENAGE GIRLS THAT I FOUNDED, EDIT, AND WRITE FOR

ROOKIE

ELSEWHERE

8tracks
instagram
twitter
i do not have a facebook page or profile.

MORE STUFF

Stylelikeu
BBC
The Colbert Report
New York Times profile
Chicago Tribune profile
Jimmy Fallon
How Was Your Week?
Bullseye with Jesse Thorn
Wait Wait...Don't Tell Me!
KCRW's Guest DJ Project

These are some of the things I've written for Rookie:

poetry
being a person is hard
being a person is nice
the rookie road trip diaries
about loneliness
lindsay weir and joan didion

Power to the people

IDEA № 89
SOCIAL MEDIA

It is perhaps no surprise that the generation born in the 1990s, raised on reality TV, performance and the idea of fame as the new global currency, would be at the forefront of exploring the potential of the new social media – virtual communities of people who exchange, create and share content on the internet.

One of the first social media platforms, Myspace, was launched in 2003 as a site for musicians, actors and artists – in effect, a cheap marketing tool for new talent. But foreseeing the potential of such sites, its founders, Chris DeWolfe and Tom Anderson, conceived it as a hybrid of social networking and the kind of personal expression enabled by personal web pages and blogs. In 2005 video-sharing site YouTube started to provide a similar kind of free-to-all platform for youth to 'broadcast yourself', as its tagline had it. Youth culture went viral, shared among peer groups and beyond by social networking sites such as Facebook, Twitter, Instagram, Pinterest, Tumblr and others.

Crucially, these various forms of social media shifted the power base away from the traditional top-down model of publishing, publicity and trend generation, and put the means of expression, and of decision-making, into the hands of youths themselves. The broader relevance of street-level trends was greatly boosted.

Social media users could select, for example, those new talents, styles, fashion labels they chose to support (and then report on) by measures important to them. The so-called Bieber effect, after the pop star Justin Bieber, saw new talents picked up, as Bieber was, by mainstream publishing and promotional companies after developing a strong following online via songs or performances that they had posted by themselves. Similarly, fashion brands too small for marketing budgets, or their own retail space, could prosper through social media word of mouth, linking commentary to online sales sites like of eBay.

Inspired by the boom online in influential bloggers, street photography and other 'user-generated content', social media could be used simply to share favoured looks too. Fashion was democratized in direction as fast-fashion retail had been in price. Fashion brands in turn not only launched their own social networks but, like fashion buyers, found it increasingly important to listen to the chatter among their customers and respond to calls for certain products or changes in behaviour, even using social media to help with the prediction of coming trends. ■

ABOVE: *The ubiquity of affordable, high-quality cameras (and cameras on smartphones) and the means to self-publish the results by way of the internet, had by the mid-2000s prompted an explosion of street style documentation and analysis.*

OPPOSITE: *Social media has provided a platform for all sorts of opinions on style from all sorts of would-be style-makers. Some, such as Tavi Gevinson, a young teenager when she started blogging, prove influential and are therefore courted by many fashion companies.*

Underwear as outerwear

IDEA Nº 90
BURLESQUE

When, as a joke, French designer Jean Paul Gaultier devised a conical bra bustier for Nana, his teddy bear, he did not expect a version to be worn as stagewear by Madonna for her 'Blond Ambition' tour of 1990. But with her doing so, the idea of underwear as outerwear was at once cemented in the popular imagination as a rebellious style. The look was quickly copied by the teen and twenty-something mainstream.

A decade later, underwear took centre-stage in less rebellious form with the revival of American burlesque. In part inspired by Baz Luhrmann's movie *Moulin Rouge* (2001), in part by the renaissance and reappraisal of striptease as a performance art – led most notably by the American performer Dita Von Teese – underwear may have gone undercover again but increasingly it aimed at a lingerie of the retro high-glamour style.

The classic lingerie styles of the 1940s and 1950s – the heyday of striptease, as well as of the Hollywood starlet – were re-imagined as more sexy than seedy: stockings, corsets, bustiers, frills and flounces, with nods to wartime pin-ups drawn by the likes of George Petty, Al Moore and Alberto Vargas. Lace and sheer fabrics – those that hinted at what lay beneath without being fully revealing – became fashion trend regulars for those wishing to experiment in the look while preserving their modesty. Crucially – while licensing authorities debated the often subtle distinction between a burlesque club and a strip club – pop cultural interest in burlesque also ushered in a new appreciation for the (in theory) empowerment of the playfully sexual and, more clearly, the distinctively feminine. The globally successful American TV series *Mad Men*, set with exacting period detail in the 1950s and 1960s, was also an influential factor in driving a shift in style that ran counter to the more unisex daily staples of jeans and T-shirts.

The foregrounding of women's underwear had wide resonance by the early 2010s, especially among pop stars (and their fans) seeking a more avant-garde or mildly subversive image, from Lady Gaga to Britney Spears, Kylie Minogue to Christina Aguilera. ∎

ABOVE: *Arguably the most influential modern striptease performer since Gypsy Rose Lee (1911–1970), Dita Von Teese's act prompted a reconsideration of corsetry and traditional lingerie during the 2000s.*

OPPOSITE: *Miss Dolly Rae and Vicky Butterfly at the Palms Hotel and Casino during the Burlesque Hall of Fame Weekend in Las Vegas, Nevada a town that has long supported the striptease arts.*

The search for the one-off

VINTAGE

The appeal of old clothing during the early 1990s was more than a newfound appeal for the second-hand. Indeed, while charity and thrift shops may have been the hunting grounds of those into vintage style, the clothes they sought were ranked with a level of sophistication lost on the long-established market for second-hand items.

Vintage clothing enthusiasts, as with other areas of vintage interest, from cars to jewellery to instruments, typically had a keen knowledge of and particular interest in period style, detail or maybe designer, in a way that saw clothes as historic artefacts. Or they rated a vintage item as belonging only to a certain stretch of, most often, the twentieth century (often those decades that predated their own birth) – merely to be second-hand or no longer available was not enough to warrant its acceptance as a vintage piece, nor was any item of obvious average or poor quality. By the twenty-first century, women's vintage focused on the pieces from the past collections of recognized designers, while menswear focused on pre-1960s military, work and sportswear, though menswear also crept towards its own new regard for the breakthrough designs of more intellectual designers like Dries Van Noten, Yohji Yamamoto, Comme des Garçons and Raf Simons.

What began as a specialist interest had by the mid-2000s, however, become another mainstream category of fashion, with high-street retailers sourcing their own selection of vintage items, specialist vintage boutiques proliferating, street markets both new and landmark – from London's Portobello Market to Paris's Marché aux Puces – seeing brisk business, and the online marketplace, eBay and Etsy notably, also providing a means for the individual both to buy and sell vintage pieces to an international customer base. Alternatively a vintage effect would be mimicked or directly copied by modern clothes manufacturers, thereby undercutting one of the key reasons for the initial interest in vintage clothing.

Vintage offered value for money: before a market for vintage clothing became widely recognized, a vintage item could be considerably cheaper than a modern counterpart, as well as being better made. Moreover, it offered an environmentally conscious means of reusing clothing that had already been made, rather than encouraging further textile production by buying new. But, in the face of increased mass production at low prices made possible by Far Eastern production, vintage primarily offered true exclusivity and the chance to wear a genuine one-off (or at least a garment one was unlikely to see anyone else wearing). Vintage provided the sartorial individualism otherwise possible only through made-to-measure, bespoke or couture clothing. ∎

ABOVE: *One Samuel Coleman, wearing a vintage suit from the 1960s, re-tailored for a better fit, shot outside the Lincoln Center during New York's fashion week in 2012. The case and hat add to the* Mad Men *style.*

OPPOSITE: *A vintage-attired member of the Hungarian Bicycle Club (with a modern bicycle) in Budapest in 2012.*

An unofficial section of the Comic-Con
2008 comic convention in San Diego,
California, saw steampunks as
Victorian 'Ghostbusters', complete
with Tesla coils and steam engines.

Yesterday meets tomorrow

IDEA № 92

STEAMPUNK

If fashion often looks to the past for inspiration or imagines what it might look like in the future, steampunk envisages a melding of the two, taking the aesthetic of the Victorian and Edwardian periods and crossing it with both the science of today and ideas of tomorrow.

In short, steampunk dresses for the world imagined by such writers as the science fiction pioneers H.G. Wells and Jules Verne, notably Verne's *20,000 Leagues Under the Sea* (1870), with its misanthropic technological genius, Captain Nemo, or captured in movies like Barry Sonnenfield's *Wild Wild West* (1999). It imagines how present-day technology might have looked had it been invented in the nineteenth century and an alternative history followed. The term 'steampunk' was coined, somewhat tongue in cheek, in the late 1980s by author K.W. Jeter, borrowing from '**cyberpunk**' but referencing the predominant Victorian technology of steam power.

Steampunk creates the clothes – and often the gadgets, or at least the real shells of imagined mechanical gadgets – that might have existed in such a future-retro science fiction world (or, in one popular sub-sect, that might have existed in a post-apocalyptic world of the kind portrayed in films such as *Mad Max* and *Waterworld*). The style is most popular in the West – where the literary genre originated – and its look closely echoes the historical period dress: top hats, frock coats, pocket watches, monocles, crinolines, long opera gloves, scarves, driving coats and goggles and – like goth, with which it shares some elements – a predominance of black. The science fiction element is based around often elaborate, carefully crafted but self-built props that are part fashion accessory, part fantasy device.

Steampunk fans mix a knowledgable appreciation for period style that a fashion interest in vintage clothing might not normally attain, with a love of dressing up in character – one reason why steampunk style proliferates more at conventions and private gatherings than on the street. ■

ABOVE AND BELOW: Neo-Victorian dress meets big goggles and arm-wear with an unspecified purpose, at the California Steampunk Convention in 2008.

Kiddy cute for grown-ups

IDEA № 93
DECORA

If cuteness is a quality many children actively seek to be free of as they aspire to being an adult, then the Japanese subculture of decora (from 'decoration') turned the tables. Originating in Tokyo's Harajuko and Shibuya fashion districts in the late 1990s and peaking in the mid-2000s, it saw grown women embracing all things childlike as a defining style.

The style was all about kawaii, or cute, and decora fashion-followers aimed to be as kawaii as possible. Bubble-gum pink or soft pastels were the preferred shades, along with clashing prints and patterns. Overtly girlish clothing, such as princess dresses, flounces and frilled skirts, undersized graphic T-shirts and oversized shoes, was worn with an excess of garish plastic accessories, from multiple bracelets to hair clips.

Attachments of a more obvious childishness, including teething rings, baby's bottles, virtual pets and other toys, were also favoured, many of them home-made or customized. A Hello Kitty or Pokémon backpack was often carried. Make-up was minimal, in keeping with the notion of childlike innocence, although facial stickers were part of the look, and hair was worn in pigtails or bunches. Everything was piled on, as though a child had been allowed to dress herself and did not know when to stop: three pairs of socks might be worn layered over each other, for example.

Indeed, although a decora look actually required some skill to assemble, the accessibility and fun of it, as well as the international sales of products by the likes of Hello Kitty, saw it emulated outside Japan, notably as a costume for cosplay (costumed role play). That, in turn, aided the evolution of a number of more rigidly rule-bound sub-styles for decora in Japan, some of them hybrids with other Tokyo subcultures: koteosa, or dark decora, was decora with a mostly black, gothic twist; and decololi, or decora-Lolita, mixed the **Lolita** style with decora's over-emphasis on plastic accessories. ■

ABOVE: *Decora style in full flow, exhibiting the decorative nature of clashing pattern, colour and texture that inspires the name. Here four students pose in Osaka's Mura district in 2004.*

Make-up into rebellion

IDEA № 94
GANGURO

The name ganguro translates literally as 'black face'. And it was no coincidence that the Japanese subculture's most famed exponent, Buriteri, nicknamed after a particularly dark soy sauce, was also a model for a Tokyo tanning salon called Blacky. Ganguro, which broke in the mid-1990s and reached a peak by the turn of the next decade, was all about extreme tanning, offset by pale hair and make-up.

This extreme tan, or its artificial recreation through the wearing of dark foundation, prefigured the Western, celebrity-driven trend of the late 2000s for deep tans. But in Japan the look, though purely fashionable for some, was different – and not only in being rare for being defined less by clothing than almost entirely by a style of make-up (although some followers of the trend did prefer platform shoes, excessive amounts of brightly coloured plastic jewellery and, for a while, the wearing of stickers on the face). Indeed, ganguro, while sometimes unconvincingly ascribed to a mimicking of African-American Hollywood actresses, was more of a social statement about, or against, traditional Japanese ideals of feminine beauty often seen as restrictive.

If these ideals revered pale skin, dark hair and fine features, which were enhanced by only a very minimal use of make-up, then ganguro pursued the opposite (in one sense a counter to the geisha aesthetic): dark skin, dyed and sometimes bleached blond or silvered hair – with perhaps a pop colour streak – and additional bold effects in make-up. These chiefly served to enhance the skin's darkness by contrast: pale, almost luminescent areas around the eye sockets, and equally pale lips, an effect often created by using concealer designed for white skin. False eyelashes and dark eyeliner – often black ink was used – completed the striking, and predominantly women's style, being part of the Japanese 'gyaru' (from the US 'gal') culture.

While clearly alternative and rebellious, especially given the respect for conformity in Japanese culture, ganguro was short-lived and localized – focused around the fashion-forward Shibuya area of Tokyo – in no small part because the Japanese media were almost entirely negative in their appraisal (sometimes equating the look with a lack of hygiene). Die-hard fans, however, developed it further with the more extreme 'yamanba', in which the tans are darker still. ■

Pure escapism

IDEA № 95
LOLITA

To Western minds at least, a street style called Lolita and involving dressing like a hyperreal version of a small girl inevitably gives rise to connotations of inappropriate child–adult relationships. Yet the Japanese Lolita style is more about covering up than exposing flesh, more about escapism and self-determination in a society in which gender codes remain strict. Like many 'dressing-up box' styles of dress, it embodies the appeal of the fantastic in fashion.

That the style shares its name with Vladimir Nabokov's novel about a middle-aged man's obsession with a 12-year 'nymphet' is a fact of which many 'Lolitas' are unaware. In fact, Lolita, the style, is based more around the Japanese cultural appreciation of the cute that saw the global reach of character merchandise such as Hello Kitty. And, contrary to the sexualization of children, it actually affects a nonsexual propriety that undercuts the oversexualized nature of fashion promotion from the late twentieth century onwards.

Lolita as a style began in Tokyo in the early 1980s, growing out of an almost competitive spirit to wear ever more outlandish outfits. Certain streets of the city's fashionable Harajuku district had been closed to traffic on Sundays and, subsequently, it became the habit of young people to gather there. In part this was to listen to street gigs, but increasingly it began to take on the form of an unofficial parade, a place to see and be seen; this was especially the case after photographer Shoichi Aoki began to document the styles he saw and then publish them in his magazine *Street*.

Lolita was just one of the Japanese style subcultures that developed in that area at that time. But it was also one of the most distinctive, taking its dress sense from the classic childrenswear of the Rococo and Victorian eras (of the kind typically found in England at the time), such as full, knee-length, bell-shaped skirts, pinafore fronts, puff-shouldered and -sleeved blouses, Alice bows or bonnets, petticoats, long socks and flat Mary Jane shoes, all given a cartoonish twist in terms of colour, print, hair and other accessories. Lolitas might carry teddy bears or porcelain dolls (again, harking back to Victoriana).

Indeed, among Japanese fashion subcultures, such has been the reach of Lolita's little-princess aesthetic – and this despite its expense – that it has found adherents outside Japan. After an initial period that prized making your own clothing, it has inspired clothing brands dedicated to it, including Baby the Stars Shine Bright, Angelic Pretty, Mary Magdalene and Innocent World (a condition to which the look perhaps aspires). It has also spawned spin-offs such as the all-black gothic Lolita, sailor, country and aristocrat Lolita and, perhaps inevitably, the so-called ero Lolita, which plays up the erotic. ∎

OPPOSITE: *Lolita, despite the name suggesting the cute and feminine, has many subgenres, including gothic Lolita (above), in which a similar style of dress is rendered in black. This, however, is enough to make them stand in stark contrast to the more everyday variety, seen here as a group in Tokyo's fashionable Harajuku district (below).*

RIGHT: *Such is the interest in Lolita fashion that, while other theatrical subcultures – the likes of steampunk or cosplay – require outfits to be home-made, Lolita is catered to by specialist clothing companies. Here a Japanese student wears designs by Angelic Pretty, in Tokyo, 2008.*

Although Japan has other subcultures that foreground the likes of bleached hair or an artificially deep tan, kogal embraces these elements alongside a schoolgirl look.

Back to school

IDEA № 96
KOGAL

Each generation of schoolchildren finds some way to subvert the school uniform – wearing the tie thin side out, rolling a regulation skirt at the top to shorten it, and so on. Few, on leaving school, would wish to revisit their uniforms as a form of subculture. Not so, however, in Japan of the mid-1990s, where kogal fashion saw young women dressing in a codified form of the classic Japanese school uniform.

'Kogal' is an anglicized term derived from 'kogyaru', a conflation of 'kokosei gyaru' or 'high school gal'; it is not a term used by the girls themselves, who refer to themselves rather as gyaru. The kogal style saw knitwear worn long and baggy, white socks worn loose and rucked and skirts worn short, in an act of defiance by the so-called original kogals of the previous decade, who were often drop-outs from expensive private schools – actual schoolgirls rather than fashion ones, for whom the wearing of a school uniform in a way counter to school regulations was to thumb a nose at authority. In some cases the look encompassed a kind of make-up-based facial tan

that prefigured the dark-faced, bleach-haired **ganguro** style.

Indeed, the kogal look was often not worn by actual students, a fact that won its adherents a degree of opprobrium from the Japanese media (as do most outsider fashion trends in Japan that deviate from the conservative norm). Kogals were considered blatant exemplars of conspicuous consumption, with designer accessories and **cell phones** being as much part of the look as the clothing, and were even accused of a pursuing a form of 'prostitution', or, more specifically, hiring out their company through dating services. Naturally the fetishistic nature of the

schoolgirl uniforms played to the media's prurience.

In reality, kogal was more likely just one of Japan's – and in particular Tokyo's – many girl or 'gal' tribes, from 'onee gals', inspired by Hollywood celebrity culture, to hime gyaru or 'princess gals', who dress in a self-consciously saccharine way inspired by fairytales. ∎

TOP AND LEFT: Possibly the most distinctive part of the kogal or schoolgirl fashion is the thick, white socks, worn pushed down to the heel, although often treated with stiffening agents like spray starch, or worn layered, to help them hold in position. Others might suggest the more eye-catching element of the dress is the skirt, hitched up so as to be won particularly short – resulting in a blend of sexiness and childishness that Western cultures might find challenging.

Reinventing the 1950s

IDEA № 97

REPRODUCTION

The reproduction of vintage clothing was, until the 1980s, largely the preserve of the cinema and theatre industries, which required it for costume dramas and other productions. Extensive research would lead to the creation of historically accurate clothing, with creative alterations to express character or reflect the needs of a specific scene.

But it took the confluence of history and artisanal making skills for reproduction, or 'repro', manufacturing to become dominated by the Japanese. The occupation of Japan by American forces at the end of World War II led local manufacturers to switch to supplying the needs of the Americans; Japanese company Big John, for example, was launched to make uniforms for them. But, unexpectedly perhaps, and aided by an influx of American pop culture, it also inspired a deep and

lasting fascination with the Americana of the 1940s and 1950s.

Access to high-quality and correctly sized clothing of that era would, however, become extremely limited in Japan in a matter of decades, especially as the original American companies more closely followed the fashions of the times or passed over to more mass manufacturing. Indeed, when, in 1988, Japanese tailor Hidehiko Yamane made a few pairs of stitch-for-stitch copies of

1950s Levi's jeans for some friends, he found sufficient demand – at home and later abroad, as repro fashion took hold outside of Japan – to start a denim business under the name of Evis (later Evisu). He even bought original 1950s shuttle looms from Levi's and insisted on the use of long-abandoned manufacturing techniques such as chain-stitching and indigo loop-dyeing.

Nor would Evis be alone. Japan's long tradition of craft weaving and its manufacturing industry's long-recognized talent for perfecting fledgling ideas of others would quickly develop to create a whole 'repro' style through the 1990s and beyond. Rare denim, workwear and military pieces in particular (available as originals only to a few, wealthy collectors) were reproduced for an international market. It was a market mostly of men, more especially inclined to be appreciative of both the utilitarian style of the postwar period and the nerdy relevance of historically accurate detail.

Japanese companies such as Buzz Rickson, Tailor-Toyo and Sugar Cane would inspire similar launches in the US, as well as the creation of reproduction lines by Levi's themselves and the other long-established companies that had driven the look originally. Indeed, by end of the first decade of the twenty-first century trawling the archive for reissues would become a fashion in itself. Niche magazines such as *Free & Easy* and *Lightning* subsequently launched to document the growing scene too. ■

Shooting fashion on the street is not new, even if in 1955 – when this image was taken, in Italy – it was still cause to draw a crowd of onlookers. Photographers like Norman Parkinson, would make shooting in public outdoor settings one of their trademarks.

Capturing the way real people dress

IDEA Nº 98
STREET PHOTOGRAPHY

It was not until the post-World War II decades that photographers – aided by new fast, affordable and lightweight point-and-shoot cameras – began documenting fashion as it was found on the street, away from catwalk presentations and designers' studios. What made this a crucial aspect of fashion's development was that, although dissemination of the images was limited, such street photography captured the way real people dressed – it was documentary photography, but focused on especially fashionable or stylish passers-by as a form of historical/social record for some, as a means of simply capturing the times' diversity of dress for others.

ABOVE: *Street photography made a professional-standard camera a fashion accessory in its own right, the latest brand or model of camera displayed as though it were the latest handbag.*

BELOW: *The pioneering street fashion photographer Bill Cunningham – shooting 'from the hip'.*

Pioneering in this field was photographer Bill Cunningham, who began shooting street fashion in 1966, soon contributing to *The New York Times* with his regular 'On the Street' page. By the 1980s, in line with the decade's explosion of international fashion brands, Amy Arbus was also shooting examples of fashionable dress she found around New York for her column in *The Village Voice* (also called 'On the Street'), although her focus was primarily on the era's distinctive style tribes and more extreme forms of dress.

It was in the 2000s that street fashion photography boomed, with widespread access to affordable, quality cameras (found even on cell phones) and with, more importantly, the internet providing a means of instantaneous publication. Pre-eminent was ex-fashion showroom manager Scott Schuman, whose blog 'The Sartorialist' kick-started a new and popular appreciation for spontaneous, stylish dressing among ordinary people, rather than just carefully groomed models or movie stars. Yvan Rodic's 'Face Hunter' blog was also influential.

Indeed, at this point street fashion photography began to have a deeper impact too, and not only on the style of more traditional fashion photography: while fashion brands have long looked to what is being worn on the street for inspiration (the 'trickle-up' theory), street fashion photography arguably broke their stranglehold on shaping major seasonal fashion trends. Street fashion photography – and, later, street fashion video – may have readily identified new cliques, but it also underscored the idea that dressing as an individual was at the root of stylishness. ∎

Two wheels good

IDEA № 99
CYCLING

When cycling became a popular pastime in the late nineteenth century it defined its own style: plus-fours prevented trousers getting caught up in gearing, while bloomers for women saved any possibility of immodesty (despite ankle-length skirts). Indeed, the uptake of cycling encouraged the support of a reform of women's clothing in particular towards the more lightweight and practical.

But it was not until the 1970s, with the advent of the cycle messenger or courier in New York and other major American cities, demand for whom rose with increased traffic congestion, that a more urban, though no less practical style grew up for the cyclist. This included fitted T-shirts and sometimes professional cycling jerseys (a choice that spilled over in breaking), Lycra shorts or rolled denim, and envelope-shaped messenger bags, which saw an immediate uptake by non-cycling street fashion.

By the late 1990s, such was the fashionability in metropolitan cities for riding a bicycle (a response to increased health and environmental awareness, as well as to traffic congestion) that cycling became a strong subculture. This took many forms – trick-riding, alleycat racing and bicycle polo – but was focused around a demand for certain kinds of bicycles, from custom-built, fixed-gear and stripped-back models to traditional, retro styles, and also a certain style. As in the previous century, in most instances the look was primarily practical. Borrowing from BMX and skate culture, preferences leaned to hard-wearing workwear, skate shoes, skinny jeans and outdoor pursuits shell jackets; it was also not unknown for some riders to have different sets of coloured wheels to match their outfits.

When cycle style became more fashionably mainstream the culture spawned bicycle cafes and clubs, events, bicycle culture magazines and books, and **reproduction** and new dedicated clothing lines from both independent companies and brand giants such as Levi's – lines that crossed skate-inspired style with high-tech, breathable, waterproof fabrics in slimline cuts. ∎

ABOVE: *Tom Simpson rides alongside Jean Stablinski during the World Road Cycling Championships in Italy in 1962. The aesthetic of cycling clothing of the sport's golden era – tight, graphically bold, logo-covered – shaped a new interest in cycle-specific clothing in the 2000s, with the revival of companies like Rapha.*

LEFT: *The cyclist as urban knight, defined by the cycle couriers of New York and, here, London, in 2009, blending skatewear with Lycra cycling shorts, worn under looser-fit shorts, with tattoos, beard and, the most important accessory of all, the fixed-wheel bicycle.*

Wearing a retro cycling top and gloves, the real status item for cycle style is less the clothing than the bicycle, the less off-the-rack the better – in this instance it is a 1980s Maggioni with Columbus SL tubing.

Style-cult clash and curation

MAGPIE STYLE

It has been called magpie style, for its readiness to borrow and radically combine looks from a host of twentieth- and twenty-first-century style tribes and trends. It has also been called 'pick and mix', while in 2010 the style anthropologist Ted Polhemus dubbed it 'the supermarket of style'.

Arguably magpie style is the fashion expression of postmodernism: a mash-up of sartorial references from historical eras, on one level knowing (only insiders might spot the references), on another level ironic (a look might combine elements from style cultures of their parents' or even grandparents' youth that would originally have been worn only by self-proclaimed enemies, such as a mod parka over a rocker's biker jacket, or punk touches with brothel creeper shoes). On a third level it is a reflection of the technological times we live in.

Indeed, this third factor is perhaps the most important. Affordable digital photography and the internet have not only allowed the wealth of pop cultural knowledge of historical style groups to grow, but also ensured that it has never been harder for new style cultures to take hold in the same way as those older, deeply influential ones did. No sooner has a clique established its own style, no matter how localized, than it will be documented and disseminated globally, then copied, either by individuals outside the clique, or – thanks to fast-fashion manufacturing – by high-street fashion retailers who take it mainstream. This in turn, of course, kills the style before it has the opportunity to mature.

More positively, the internet has also allowed global street style photography – the documenting of the dress of private individuals on the street – to flourish, thereby encouraging the development of a more personal style than one simply prescribed by an idea of some tribal uniform. Rather than the sometimes cartoon-like effects of nostalgic **revivalism**, the more sophisticated magpie style embraces one's own personal sampling, editing, curation and assembly of clothing resonating from the past giving it new life in the present. ∎

ABOVE: *French star Vanessa Paradis mixes a long floaty dress with tough leather for the Chanel haute couture show in Paris in early 2012.*

LEFT: *Magpie style allows the exploring of often extreme contrasts in clothing styles, as here where the hairstyle, jacket and flared trousers seem to have come from very different worlds.*

OPPSITE: *Model Kristina Salinovic being snapped during Paris Fashion Week in July 2011.*

Further Reading

Books

Aoki, Shoichi. *Fruits*, Phaidon Press, 2001.

——. *Fresh Fruits*, Phaidon Press, 2005.

Bar Ann with Peter Walk. *The Sloane Ranger Handbook*, Ebury Press, 1982.

Birnbach, Lisa. *The Official Preppy Handbook*, Workman Publishing Company, 1980.

Brown, Tim. *The Wigan Casino Years: Northern Soul; The Essential Story 1973–81*, Outta Sight Limited, 2010.

Brunel, Charlotte and Bruno Collin. *The T-Shirt Book*, Tashen, 2002.

Bushell, Garry. *Dance Craze: Rude Boys on the Road*, Countdown Books, 2011.

Cogan, Brian. *The Encyclopaedia of Punk*, Greenwood Press, 2006.

Constantine, Elaine and Gareth Sweeney. *Northern Soul*, Virgin, 2013.

Cunnigham, Bill. *Facades*, Penguin Press, 1978.

Eddington, Richard. *Sent from Coventry: The Chequered Past of Two Tone*, Independent Music Press, 2004.

Farren, Mick. *The Black Leather Jacket*, Plexus Publishing, 2008.

Friedrichs, Horst A. *Cycle Style*, Prestel, 2012.

Gale, Nathan. *Art & Sole: Contemporary Sneaker Design: Contemporary Sneaker Art & Design*, Laurence King Publishing, 2008.

Hebdige, Dick. *Subculture: The Meaning of Style*, Routledge, 1979.

Hewitson, Dave and Jay Montessori. *80s Casuals: The Fashion of an Urban, Working Class Culture, with a Love of Training Shoes and Designer Sportwear*, Eighties Casuals, 2010.

Marsh, Graham. *Denim From Cowboys to Catwalks: A History of the World's Most Legendary Fabric*, Aurum Press, 2005.

NYLON Magazine, *Street View: The New Nylon Book of Global Style*. Universe Publishing, 2010.

Polhemus, Ted. *Street Style*, PYMCA, 2010.

Rawlings, Terry. *Mod: A Very British Phenomenon*, Omnibus Press, 2001.

Rodic, Yvan. *Facehunter*, Prestel Press, 2010.

——. *Travels with Facehunter: Street Style from Around the World*, Running Press Book Publishers, 2013.

Schuman, Scott. *The Sartorialist*, Penguin Books, 2009.

——. *The Sartorialist: Closer*, Particular Books, 2012.

Sims, Josh. *Cult Streetwear*, Laurence King Publishing, 2010.

——. *Icons of Men's Style*, Laurence King Publishing, 2011.

Sims, Josh with Douglas Gunn and Roy Luckett. *Vintage Menswear*, Laurence King Publishing, 2012.

Smits, Kim with Matthijs Matt. *Custom Kicks: Personalized Footwear*, Laurence King Publishing, 2008.

——. *Tees: The Art of the T-Shirt*, Laurence King Publishing, 2009.

Worsley, Harriet. *100 Ideas that Changed Fashion*, Laurence King Publishing, 2011.

Films

Accattone, directed by Pier Paolo Pasolini, 1961. (La Dolce Vita)

L'Assassino, directed by Elio Petri, 1961. (La Dolce Vita)

Blade Runner, directed by Ridley Scott, 1982. (Cyberpunk)

Blue Hawaii, directed by Norman Taurog, 1961. (Surf Culture)

The Blackboard Jungle, directed by Richard Brooks, 1955. (Teen Cinema)

Boogie Bones, directed by Valery Todorovsky, 2008. (Stilyagis)

The Breakfast Club, directed by John Hughes, 1985. (Teen Cinema, Preppy)

Breakdance, directed by Joel Silberg, 1984. (Breaking)

Broken Blossoms, directed by D.W. Griffith, 1919. (Teen Cinema)

The Cabinet of Dr Caligari, directed by Robert Wiene, 1920. (Goth)

The Cycle Savages, directed by Bill Brame, 1969. (Biker Culture)

La Dolce Vita, directed by Federico Fellini, 1960. (La Dolce Vita)

Easy Rider, directed by Dennis Hopper, 1969. (Biker Culture, Psychedelia)

8 ½, directed by Federico Fellini, 1963. (La Dolce Vita)

Fame, directed by Alan Parker, 1980. (Aerobics Style)

Fast Times at Ridgemont High, directed by Amy Heckerling, 1982. (Teen Cinema)

Flashdance, directed by Adrian Lyne, 1983. (Aerobics Style)

Foxy Brown, directed by Jack Hill, 1974. (Funk)

Giant, directed by George Stevens, 1956. (Jeans)

Gidget, directed by Paul Wendkos, 1959. (Teen Cinema)

Go Johnny, Go!, directed by Paul Londres, 1959. (Teen Cinema)

High School Confidential!, directed by Jack Arnold, 1958. (Teen Cinema)

Joy Ride, directed by Edward Bernds, 1958. (Teen Cinema)

Love Finds Andy Hardy, directed by George B. Seitz, 1938. (Teen Cinema)

Mad Max, directed by George Miller, 1979. (Cyberpunk)

The Matrix, directed by Andy Wachowski, 1999. (Cyberpunk)

Metropolis, directed by Fritz Lang, 1927. (Goth)

The Misfits, directed by John Huston, 1961. (Jeans, Androgyny)

Moulin Rouge, directed by Baz Luhrmann, 2001. (Burlesque)

The Night Porter, directed by Liliana Cavani, 1974. (Androgyny)

Nosferatu, directed by F.W. Murnau, 1922. (Goth)

Pretty in Pink, directed by Howard Deutsch, 1986. (Teen Cinema, Preppy)

Quadrophenia, directed by Franc Roddam, 1979. (The Mod, Revivalism)

Rebel Without a Cause, directed by Nicholas Ray, 1955. (Teen Cinema, Jeans, Customization)

RoboCop, directed by Paul Verhoeven, 1987. (Cyberpunk)

Rocco and his Brothers, directed by Lucchino Visconti, 1960. (La Dolce Vita)

Rosemary's Baby, directed by Roman Polanski, 1968. (Androgyny)

Saturday Night Fever, directed by John Badham, 1977. (Disco)

Shaft, directed by Gordon Parks, 1971. (Funk)

Singles, directed by Cameron Crowe, 1992. (Grunge)

Sixteen Candles, directed by John Hughes,1984. (Teen Cinema)

St Elmo's Fire, directed by Joel Schumacher, 1985. (Teen Cinema)

Stowaway, directed by William A. Seiter, 1936. (Teen Cinema)

A Streetcar Named Desire, directed by Elia Kazan, 1951. (Bodybuilding)

Super Fly, directed by Gordon Parks Jr., 1972. (Funk)

The Terminator, directed by James Cameron, 1984. (Cyberpunk)

Three the Hard Way, directed by Gordon Parks Jr., 1974. (Funk)

Victor Victoria, directed by Blake Edwards, 1982. (Androgyny)

West Side Story, directed by Jerome Robbins and Robert Wise, 1957. (Gang Culture)

The Wild One, directed by Laslo Benedek, 1953. (Teen Cinema, Biker Culture)

The Wizard of Oz, directed by Victor Fleming, 1939. (T-Shirt Graphics)

Yesterday, Today and Tomorrow, directed by Vittorio De Sica, 1963. (La Dolce Vita)

Index

Picture Credits

2 Shoichi Aoki; 8 Frank Monaco/Rex Features 9(top) Bruce Davidson/Magnum Photos; 9 (bottom) Ewen Spencer; 10 (top) Rob Verhorst/Redferns/Getty Images; 10 (bottom) Bettmann/CORBIS; 11 Fin Costello/Redferns/Getty Images; 12 Roger-Viollet/Topfoto; 13 Marie Hansen/Time Life Pictures/Getty Images; 14 Steve Forrest/Rex Features 15 Corbis; 16 Roger Mayne/Mary Evans Picture Library; 17 Joseph McKeown/Getty Images 18 (top) Hulton Archive/Getty Images; 18 (bottom) Michael Ochs Archives/Getty Images; 19 David Redfern/Redferns/Getty Images; 20 Wayne Miller/Magnum Photos 21 Col Pics/Everett/Rex Features; 22 (top) MONDADORI PORTFOLIO 22 (bottom) George Konig/Rex Features; 23 TopFoto 24 Pictorial Press Ltd/Alamy; 25 (top) Leonie Morse; 25 (bottom) Homer Sykes/Alamy; 26 (top) Everett Collection/Rex Features; 26 (bottom) Danny Lyon/Magnum Photos; 27 BRIAN MOODY/Rex Features; 28 (top) Ted Polhemus/PYMCA; 28 (bottom) FRANK MONACO/Rex Features; 29 Popperfoto/Getty Images; 30 (top) George Konig/Rex Features; 30 (bottom) Peter Francis/PYMCA; 31 David McEnery/Rex Features; 32(top) Hulton Archive/Getty Images; 32 (bottom) Keystone-France/Gamma-Keystone via Getty Images; 33 RIAMA-PATHE-GRAY/ASTOR-AIP/THE KOBAL COLLECTION; 34 (top) Bettmann/CORBIS; 34 (bottom) Ted Polhemus/PYMCA; 35 Bettmann/CORBIS; 36 (top) SIPA PRESS/Rex Features; 36 (bottom) Peter Stackpole/Time & Life Pictures/Getty Images; 37 J. Baylor Roberts/National Geographic/Getty Images; 38 (top) Ross Kirton/eyevine; 38 Charles Fenno Jacobs//Time Life Pictures/Getty Images; 39 Ester Segarra/ Blackthorn Pictures; 40 (bottom) Bob Willoughby/Redferns/Getty Images; 41 Michael Ochs Archives/Getty Images; 42 (top) Keystone/Getty Images; 42 (bottom) Bruce Davidson/Magnum Photos; 43 Burt Glinn/Magnum Photos; 44 Bruno Barbey/Magnum Photos; 45 (top) Photo ITAR-TASS/Red Arrow; 45 (bottom) Everett Collection/Rex Features; 46 The Advertising Archives; 47 ROLF HAYO/Rex Features; 48 (top) Photograph by John Witzig-johnwitzig.com.au; 48 (bottom) Hulton-Deutsch Collection/CORBIS; 49 (top) Michael Ochs Archives/Getty Images;49(bottom) Nicolas LE CORRE/Gamma-Rapho via Getty Images; 50 (top) Inge Morath/The Inge Morath Foundation/Magnum Photos; 50 (bottom) Patrick Zachmann/Magnum Photos; 51 Hulton Archive/Getty Images; 52 Liat Chen/PYMCA; 53 GIANCARLO/Rex Features; 54 Bert Hardy/Getty Images; 55 John Downing/Getty Images; 56 (top) Mr Hartnett/PYMCA; 56 (Bottom) Michele Poorman/PYMCA; 57 David Graves/Rex Features; 58 Steve McCurry/Magnum Photos; 59 Mr Hartnett/PYMCA; 60 Topham Picturepoint/Topfoto; 61 (top) David Hurn/Magnum Photos; 61 (bottom) CSU Archv/Everett/Rex Features; 62 (top) Tim Rooke/Rex Features; 62 (bottom) Andy Butterton/PA Archive/Press Association Images; 63 David Montgomery/Getty Images; 64 Rex Features; 65 (top L-R) Elizabeth Lippman/The New York Times/Redux/eyevine; Arnaldo Magnani/Getty Images; Elizabeth Lippman/The New York Times/Redux/eyevine; 65 (middle L-R) Brian Sweeney/PYMCA; Pav Modelski/PYMCA; James Lange/PYMCA; 65 (bottom L-R) Ted Polhemus/PYMCA; Dan Wilton/PYMCA; Alan Wilson/Alamy; 66 (top) Bruce Davidson/Magnum Photos; 66 (bottom) Ted Polhemus/PYMCA; 67 Garry Rawlings/PYMCA; 68 (top) Chris Morris/Rex Features; 68 (bottom) KEYSTONE Pictures USA/eyevine; 69 Terence Donovan Archive/Getty Images; 70 Denis Cameron/Rex Features; 71 Jack Manning/New York Times Co./Getty Images; 72 Mark Henderson/PYMCA; 73 (top) Nikos Economopoulos/Magnum Photos; 73 (bottom) Liz Johnson-Artur; 74 Ted Polhemus/PYMCA;75 John G Byrne/PYMCA; 76 Toni Tye/PYMCA; 77 (top) Lynn Goldsmith/Corbis; 77 (bottom) Ebet Roberts/Redferns/Getty Images; 78 Dean Belcher/PYMCA; 79 (top) Phoenix J Bay/PYMCA; 79(bottom) Chris Steele-Perkins/Magnum Photos; 80 (top) WARNER BROS/THE KOBAL COLLECTION; 80 (bottom) Everett Collection/Rex Features; 81 Allan Tannenbaum/Sohoblues.com; 82 Ewen Spencer; 83 (top) Ewen Spencer; 83 (bottom) ullsteinbild/TopFoto; 84 (left)

Andre Csillag/Rex Features; 84 (right) Ted Polhemus/PYMCA; 85 (top) Popperfoto/Getty Images; 85 (bottom) Ted Polhemus/PYMCA; 86 Roger BAMBER/Rex Features; 87 Roger Bamber/Rex Features; 88 Julian Broad/Exclusive by Getty Images; 89 Dennis Stock/Magnum Photos; 90 (top) PARAMOUNT/THE KOBAL COLLECTION/BOWER, HOLLY; 90 (bottom) Allan Tannenbaum/Sohoblues.com, 91 (both) Allan Tannenbaum/Sohoblues.com; 92 Mike Hollist/Daily Mail/Rex; 93 Nils Jorgensen/Rex Features; 94 (both) Rebecca Lewis; 95 Ewen Spencer; 96 Richard Braine/PYMCA; 97 Simon Wheatley/PYMCA; 98 Steve Schapiro/Corbis; 99 (top) Courtesy of Jamel Shabazz; 99 (bottom) BRENDAN BEIRNE/Rex Features; 100 (top) Liz Johnson-Artur; 100 (bottom) Ben Margot/AP/Press Association Images; 101 Lawrence Watson/PYMCA; 102 (top) Mr Hartnett/PYMCA; 102 (bottom) Janette Beckman/PYMCA; 103 Laurence Watson/PYMCA; 104 Suki Coe/Corbis; 105 (top) Tim Scott/PYMCA; 105 (bottom) Francisca Pinochet/PYMCA; 106 (top) Oliver Grove/PYMCA; 106 (bottom) Neil Hall/Rex Features; 107 Simon Wheatley/PYMCA; 108 Mr Hartnett/PYMCA; 109 (top) Mr Hartnett/PYMCA; 109 (bottom) Ted Polhemus/PYMCA; 110 Estevan Oriol/PYMCA; 111 Edward Le Poulin/Corbis; 112 (top) (c) Adrian Boot/urbanimage.tv; 112 (bottom) Liz Johnson-Artur; 113 (c) Wayne Tippetts/ urbanimage.tv; 114 (top) Ted Polhemus/PYMCA; 114 (bottom) Graham Smith/PYMCA; 115 Rex Features; 116 Christian Couzens/PYMCA; 117 Suzi Ewing/PYMCA; 118 Giles Moberly/PYMCA; 119 Janette Beckman/Getty Images; 120 (top) ABACA PRESS/ABACA USA/Press Association Images; 120(bottom) Mikey Thompson/PYMCA; 121 Janette Beckman/PYMCA; 122 (top) Roger Viollet/Bridgeman Art; 122 (bottom) Scott Houston/Sygma/Corbis; 123 Estevan Oriol/PYMCA; 124 (top) Ted Polhemus/PYMCA; 124 (bottom) Juno/PYMCA; 125 Mr Hartnett/PYMCA; 126 (top) David Swindells/PYMCA; 126 (bottom) Francesco Castaldo; 127 (both) Adam Friedman/PYMCA; 128 PA Photos/Topfoto; 129 Adrian Fisk/PYMCA; 130 Fairchild Photo Service; 131 (Top) Françoise Huguier/Agence VU; 131 (bottom) Keystone/Getty Images; 132 (top) David Corio/PYMCA; 132 (bottom) Wugie; 133 Jon Ingledew/PYMCA 134 Photography Steve Johnston, The I-D One Issue, September 1980; 135 (first row L-R) Bauer Publishing; Photography, Mark Lebon, Cover Star, Madonna, i-D, The SeXsense Issue, 1984; Dazed and Confused; Les Inrockuptibles; Sleazenation/pymca.com 135 (second row L-R) Dazed and Confused; Les Inrockuptibles; Ray Gun Collection; Shoichi Aoki; Bauer Publishing 135 (third row L-R) Ray Gun Collection; Dazed and Confused; Sleazenation/pymca.com; Les Inrockuptibles; Shoichi Aoki 135 (fourth row L-R) Sleazenation/pymca.com; Ray Gun Collection; Bauer Publishing; Dazed and Confused; Ray Gun Collection 136 Mr Hartnett/PYMCA; 137 (top) Campbell Allan/PYMCA; 137 (bottom) Liat Chen/PYMCA; 138 Soughan & Pentleton/PYMCA; 139 (top) Courtesy of Jamel Shabazz; 139 (bottom) Startraks Photo/Rex Features; 140 (top) Mondadori Portfolio; 140 (bottom) Mondadori Portfolio/Egizio Fabbrici; 141 Mondadori Portfolio/Egizio Fabbrici; 142 Owen Franken/CORBIS; 143 (top) Stephanie Pilick/Press Association Images; 143 (bottom) Romano Cagnoni/Getty Images; 144 Elliott Landy/Magnum Photos; 145 (top) David Robertson/PYMCA; 145 Matt Cardy/Getty Images; 146 (top) AAP AUSTRALIAN ASSOCIATED PRESS/AAP/Press Association Images; 146 (bottom) Leonard Freed/Magnum Photos; 147 PA Photos/Topfoto; 148 Starfile/All Action/EMPICS Entertainment; 149 (top) Moviestore Collection/Rex Features; 149 (bottom) Kyle Ericksen/CondeNast/Corbis; 150 (left) Mr Hartnett/PYMCA; 150 (right) Everett Collection/Rex Features; 151 (left) James Lange/PYMCA; 151 (right) Frazer Harrison/Getty Images; 152 Billa/Every Night; 153 David Swindells/PYMCA; 154 Lawrence Watson/PYMCA; 155 Kevin Cummins/Getty Images; 156 (top) Mick Hutson/Redferns/Getty Images; 156 (bottom) Mr Hartnett/PYMCA; 157 Mr Hartnett/PYMCA; 158 (top) KMazur/WireImage/Getty Images; 158 (bottom) Chris Jackson/

Getty Images; 159 Splash News/Corbis; 160 Daniel Biskup/laif/Camerapress; 161 Mark Henderson/PYMCA; 162 Jennifer Taylor/Corbis; 163 Liat Chen/PYMCA; 164 (Top) Nick Cunard/PYMCA; 164 (bottom) Joe Bailey (Rider: Vinnie Hunter); 165 Nick Cunard/PYMCA; 166 Alex Segre/Alamy; 167 (both) Britta Pedersen/DPA/Press Association Images; 168 Neville Elder/Blackthorn Pictures; 169 Joe Plimmer/Blackthorn Pictures; 170 (both) Ewen Spencer; 171 The Sun/N.I. Syndication; 172 Justin Sutcliffe/Blackthorn Pictures; 173 (top) Ted Polhemus/PYMCA; 173 (bottom) Francisca Pinochet/PYMCA; 174 Simon Pentleton/PYMCA; 175 (top) Neil Massey/Getty Images; 175 (bottom) Jim Saah/Jimsaah.com; 176 (top) Mr Hartnett/PYMCA; 176 (bottom) Nick Cunard/PYMCA; 177 Dean Chalkley/PYMCA; 178 (top) Francisca Pinochet/PYMCA; 178 (bottom) Nicola Okin Frioli; 179 Charlie Mahoney/Corbis; 180 (top) Robert Cianflone/Getty Images; 180 (bottom) Ray Tang/Rex Features; 181 (top) Yui Mok/PA Archive/Press Association Images; 181 (bottom) Cameron Spencer/Getty Images; 182 (top) Trevor Moore/Landmark Media; 182 (bottom) David Dagley/Rex Features; 183 Models: Joy & Lilah modelling Atsuko Kudo, photograph by Nadya Lev; 184 Tavi Gevinson; 185 Rex Features; 186 Neville Elder/Blackthorn Pictures; 187 Gareth Cattermole/Getty Images; 188 Yasmine Soiffer/Redux/eyevine; 189 Mauricio Abreu/JAI/Corbis; 190 Neville Elder/Blackthorn Pictures; 191 (both) Mark Berry/Blackthorn Pictures; 192 Ben Knight/PYMCA; 193 JapaneseStreets.com/Kjeld Duits; 194 Shoichi Aoki 195 Eriko Sugita/Reuters/Corbis; 196 (top) Shoichi Aoki; 196 (bottom) JapaneseStreets.com/Kjeld Duits; 197 JapaneseStreets.com/Kjeld Duits; 198 Claude Estebe; 199 (top) Nick Cunard/PYMCA; 199 (bottom) Iain Masterton/Alamy; 200 NARA; 201 Evisu; 202 Archivio Cameraphoto Epoche/Getty Images; 202 (top) Caroline McCredie/Getty Images; 202 Andrew Lichtenstein/Corbis; 204 (top) Offside/L'Equipe; 204 (bottom) from the series "London Couriers" Iorgis Matyassy 2009;205 Horst Friedrichs/Anzenberger/Eyevine; 206 (top) Tony Barson/Getty Images; 206 (bottom) Mr Hartnett/PYMCA; 207 Wayne Tippetts/Rex Features

Acknowledgements

The author would like to thank Tom Broadbent for picture research and Roger Fawcett-Tang for design, as well as Sophie Wise and all the team at Laurence King Publishing. Thanks also to the numerous photographers who generously contributed to the book.

LAURENCE KING

Published in 2014 by
Laurence King Publishing Ltd
361–373 City Road
London EC1V 1LR

e-mail: enquiries@laurenceking.com
www.laurenceking.com

This book was designed and produced by
Laurence King Publishing Ltd, London.

A catalogue record for this book is available
from the British Library.

ISBN: 978-1-78067-341-7

Book design: Struktur Design
Original series design: TwoSheds Design
Picture research: Tom Broadbent
Senior editor: Sophie Wise

Typeset in Swift and Gotham
Printed in China